Biking The Great Lakes Islands

A Guide to Biking Seven Islands in the Great Lakes

Kathleen &
Lawrence Abrams

Entwood Publishing
P.O. Box 268
Wausau, WI 54401

Biking the Great Lakes Islands

Published by Entwood Publishing
P.O. Box 268, Wausau, WI 54401

Printed in the United States of America

All photos by Lawrence Abrams

Library of Congress Cataloging in Publication Data

Abrams, Kathleen S.
Biking the Great Lakes Islands.

1. Bicycle touring--Great Lakes Region--Guidebooks. 2. Great Lakes Region--Description and travel--Guidebooks. I. Abrams, Lawrence F. II. Title. GV1045.5.G74A27 1985 917.7 84-82014
ISBN 0-9605978-1-6

For Nathaniel

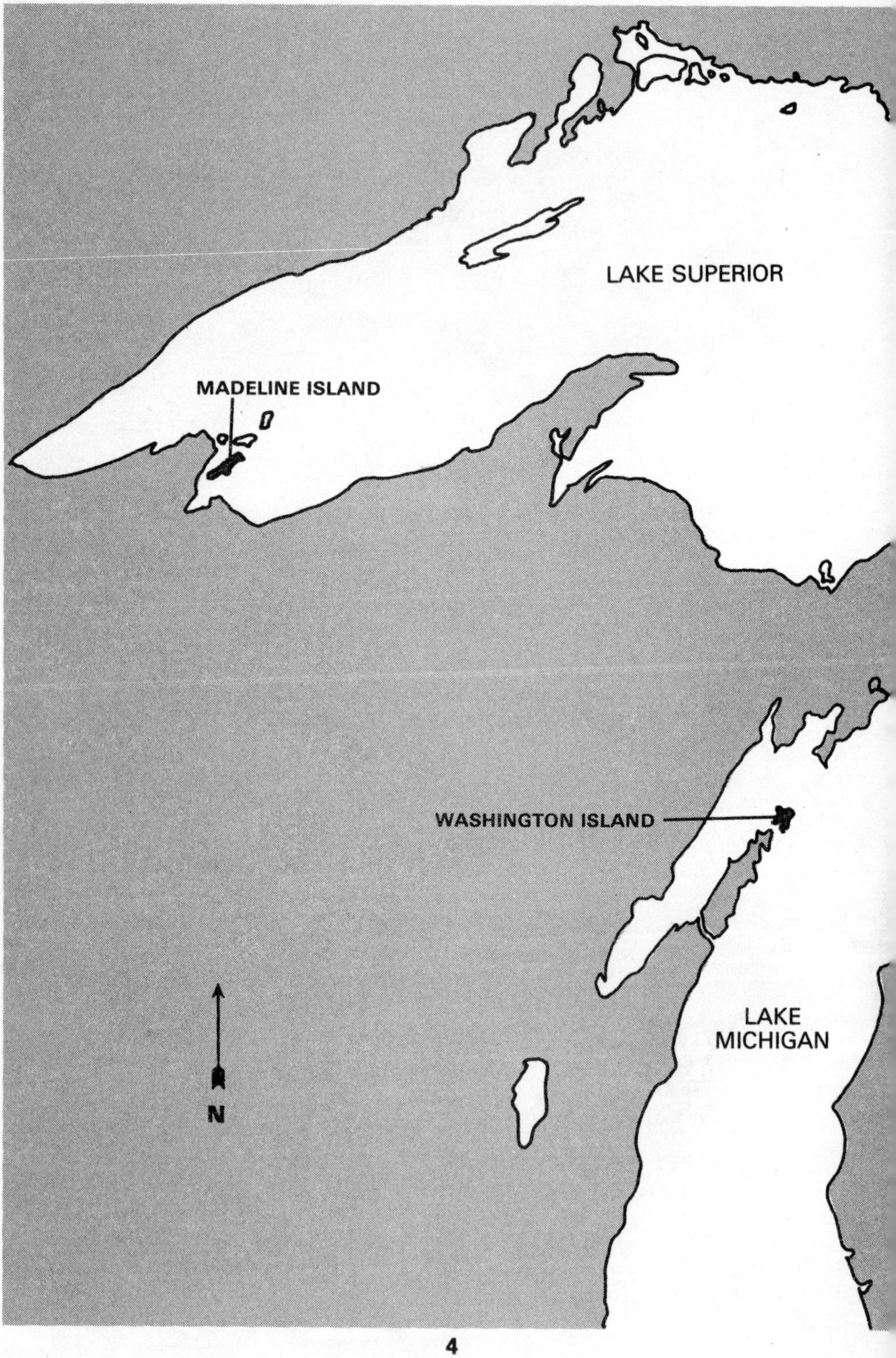
LAKE SUPERIOR
MADELINE ISLAND
WASHINGTON ISLAND
LAKE
MICHIGAN
N

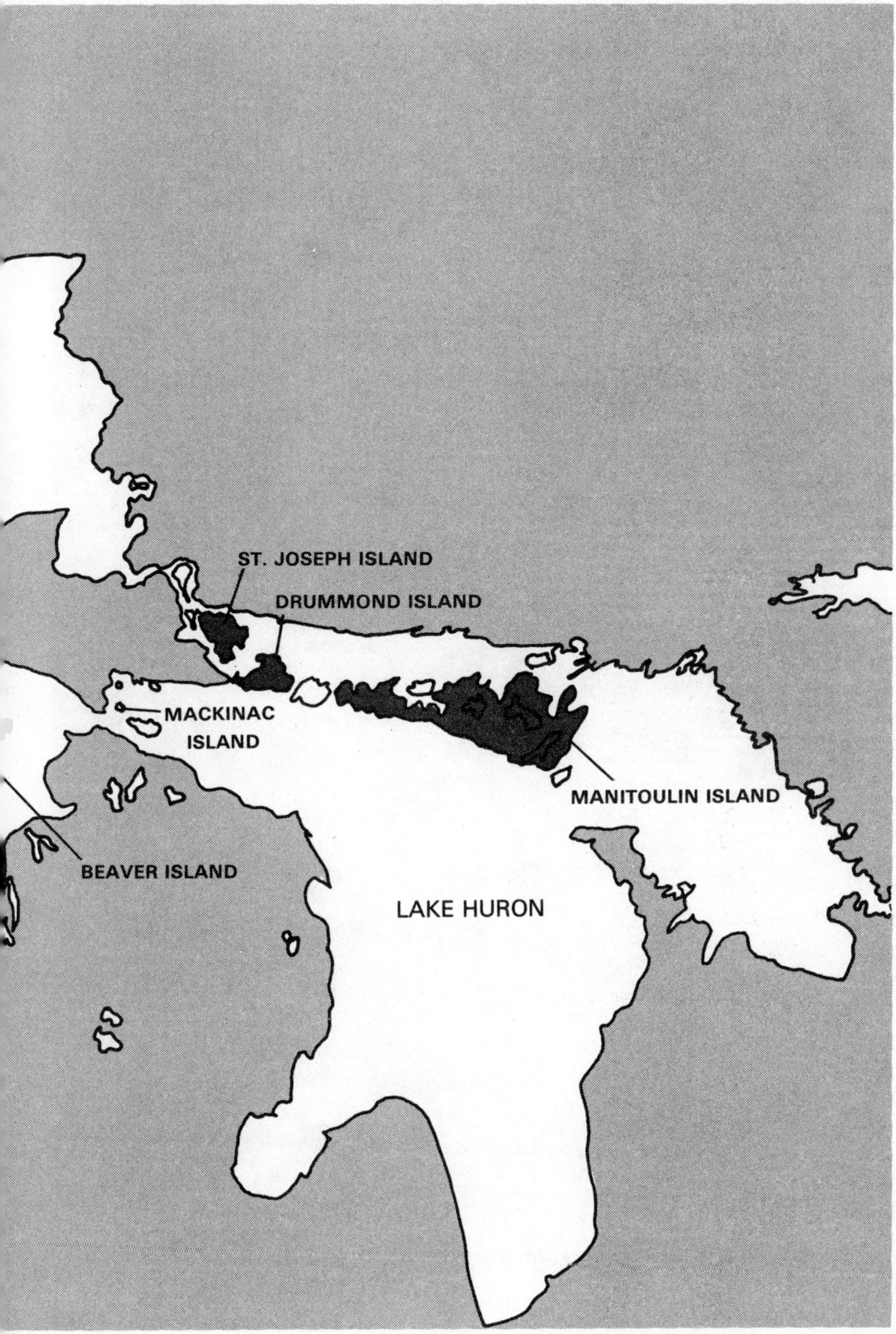
ST. JOSEPH ISLAND
DRUMMOND ISLAND
MACKINAC
ISLAND
MANITOULIN ISLAND
BEAVER ISLAND
LAKE HURON

Larry enjoys a long, even grade through dense wilderness.

Table of Contents

Introduction

Isolated from the routine rhythms of mainland life, islands radiate a special attraction. Remote, private places, they offer opportunities for reflection and relaxation. Time seems to stand still - or at least move at half the pace - when you visit an island.

Biking provides similar opportunities for reflection and relaxation. While your body speeds up as you ride a bike, your mind slows down; you can spin along wrapped in an island of thought that isolates you from the rest of the world. On a bike, as on an island, you set your own rhythms.

For that reason, when we thought about where to spend our summer biking, we chose to tour islands. Their special appeal seemed appropriate for our biking adventure. We decided to bike seven islands in the Great Lakes, ranging from Madeline Island in Lake Superior, east to Manitoulin in Canada's Lake Huron. In between, we biked Washington and Beaver islands in Lake Michigan, Mackinac and Drummond islands in Lake Huron and St. Joseph Island, a Canadian island in the passageway between Lake Huron and Lake Superior.

Although the atmosphere on these islands ranged from bustling tourist activity on Mackinac to primitive wilderness on Beaver, all seven islands shared some similar features. As bikers, we most appreciated the quiet roads. Driving seemed to be kept to a minimum on these islands. Sometimes we biked for several hours on good, paved roads but met only one or two cars.

Traffic also moved slowly on these island roads. One reason for this may be that distances are shorter on islands, so people can take more time traveling from place to place. The condition of the roads may also contribute to slow moving traffic. On some islands, especially Beaver and St. Joseph, we found we could travel the dirt roads almost as fast on bikes as in a car.

At times the lack of traffic made us feel as though we were pedaling on designated bike routes. We had the entire road to ourselves and imagining that cars were prohibited altogether was easy. But island biking is even better than pedaling on designated bike routes. On islands you are not confined to specific trails. You can choose your own routes - follow whatever interesting road appeals to you - and still enjoy the serenity of biking along low-traffic routes.

We found another unexpected advantage to biking these island roads. Although many of our routes took us past farms and cottages, we were never chased by barking dogs. We have often been harrassed by barking canines and we know that dogs "on the loose" can be a threat to bikers along rural routes. But on this island biking adventure we did not meet any aggressive dogs. Maybe, we speculated, island life relaxes dogs as well as people. Although we can't promise that your island bike trips will also be free of canine harrassment, we do wish you an experience similar to our own.

Quiet roads are definitely a plus for island biking, but we found other advantages, too. One especially appealing feature is the constant closeness to water. On an island most roads lead to a beach, and the variety of isolated beaches is one of the things we remember most about biking on these seven islands. We planned our routes to take advantage of this special attraction. Each day, with lunch safely stowed in our bike packs, we set off for a sunny stretch of sandy beach. Like the roads, these beaches were usually uncrowded, and often we were the only people enjoying that special feeling of water-cooled sand under our feet.

That closeness to the water also contributes to another advantage of island biking: lake breezes keep the islands' air temperature cool and help make the weather comfortable for biking even in those cloudless days of late summer. The weather, scenery and slower pace all combine to make island biking especially appealing.

To help you enjoy the special features of island biking we have planned tours along some of the most scenic roads on these seven islands: Madeline, Washington, Beaver, Mackinac, Drummond, St. Joseph and Manitoulin. Many of these routes take you to historical or geographical places of interest. Others find their appeal in quiet country settings.

These tours range from three mile routes that you can take before or after a day's drive to fifty mile routes planned for long distance touring. Most of the routes on each island interconnect, so you can adapt them for bike tours that fit your time schedule and ability.

Setting aside one summer to bike these islands, we drove to each island, then explored it by bike. We have personally biked every mile of the routes described in this book. You may choose to bike the islands all in one summer as we did, or select from a variety of other alternatives. You may bike only one island during a summer vacation or enjoy a few routes on a long weekend. However you use the routes described here, we think you will enjoy the experience of biking these Great Lakes islands.

Keeping the varied skills and interests of bikers in mind, we have planned these routes for dedicated tourers as well as for those people who like to get a little exercise while they are on an auto trip. You can use these routes for short jaunts from your motel room or abandon your car altogether for one or more days of bike touring. For the longer routes, we have offered suggestions for overnight accommodations. You may connect short routes for longer bike trips or use a pick-up vehicle to break up longer routes. This guide is easily adaptable to your biking skills and interests.

In addition to the routes themselves, we have included information on bikes, equipment, clothing, safety and maintenance which we hope will help adequately prepare you for biking the islands. This information comes directly from our experiences in biking these islands. It is not meant to be a comprehensive manual on equipment and maintenance; rather we intend it as a few tips from those of us who have biked these routes to you as you prepare for your island adventure. Those tips, combined with detailed maps and discussions of each tour make this a complete guide to biking the Great Lakes islands.

With this guide, we also send a biker's blessing. To all of you who share our interest in biking, may you enjoy these routes as much as we did and, as you begin your island adventure. . .

"May the wind always be at your back."

Kathy takes a rest from biking on Manitoulin.

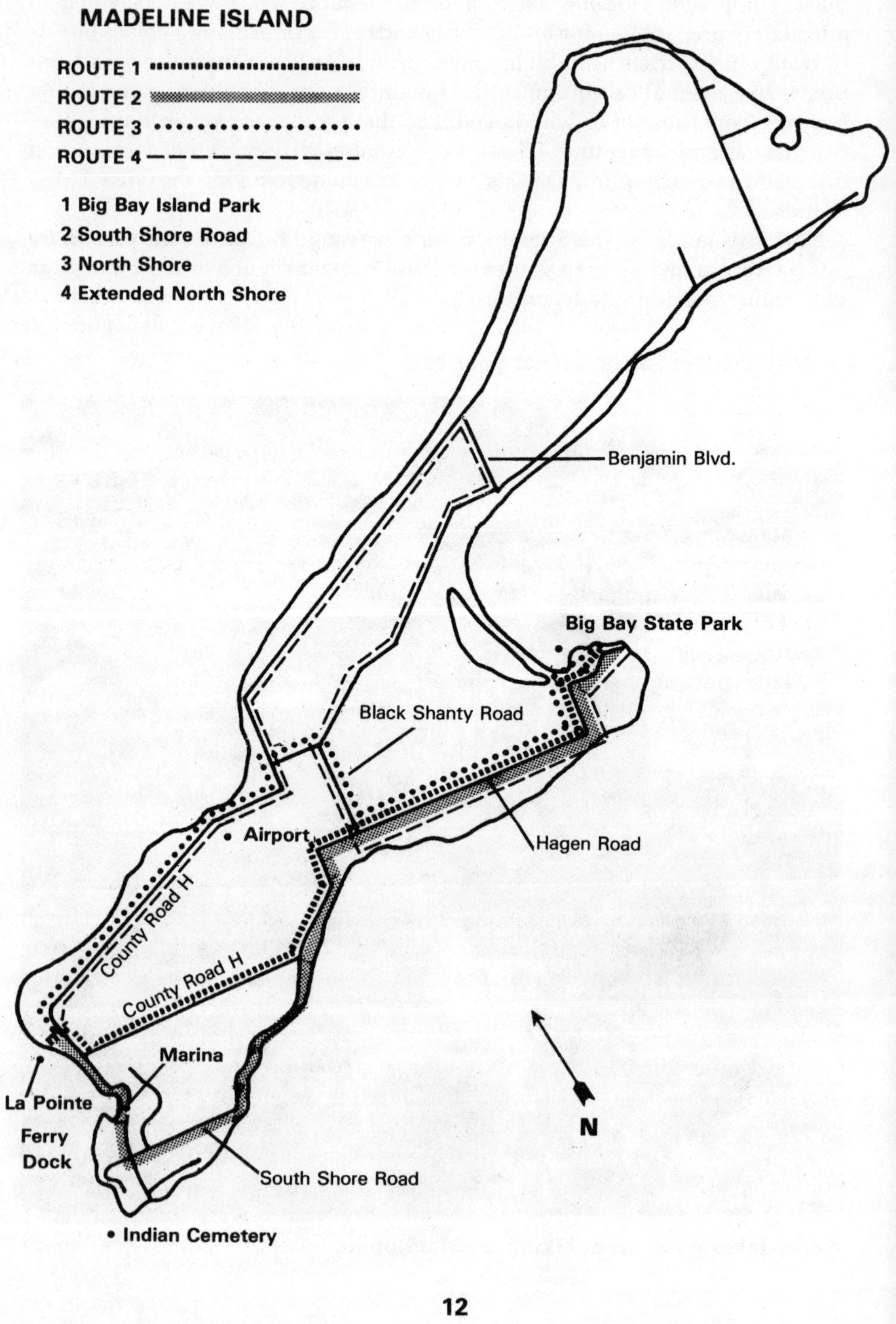
MADELINE ISLAND
ROUTE 1
ROUTE 2
ROUTE 3
ROUTE 4
1 Big Bay Island Park
2 South Shore Road
3 North Shore
4 Extended North Shore
Benjamin Blvd.
Big Bay State Park
Black Shanty Road
Airport
Hagen Road
County Road H
County Road H
Marina
La Pointe
Ferry
Dock
South Shore Road
Indian Cemetery
N

Madeline Island

Located in Lake Superior's Chequamegon Bay, Madeline Island is fourteen miles long and three miles wide. With 14,000 acres it is the largest island in the Apostle Islands, a cluster of twenty-two islands scattered off the tip of the Bayfield Peninsula. In 1970, twenty of these islands were designated the Apostle Islands National Lakeshore, but Madeline, with a winter population of about two hundred people, was excluded. Today it is the only developed island in the archipelago.

A car ferry from the charming village of Bayfield, Wisconsin takes you to La Pointe, the only settlement on the island. The ferry makes the 2.6 mile run hourly during the tourist season. Fare for a bike and rider is $5.00 round trip; for about $4.00 more, you can also take your car. But the island is easy biking, and many people leave their cars on the mainland and spend the day on the island, transported by their bikes alone. On a bike you can savor the quiet charm of La Pointe, experience the remoteness of the island's wilderness interior and glimpse the history of the island's development.

Madeline Island is named for the daughter of Ojibway Chief White Crane. For her marriage to Michel Cadotte, a French fur trader, the Indian princess traveled by canoe to Sault Ste. Marie, the site of the nearest mission. During the wedding ceremony the priest gave her the Christian name Madeline. When Madeline and Michel returned to the island, Chief White Crane, thankful for his daughter's safe return, renamed the island Madeline in her honor.

Like many other islands in the Great Lakes, Madeline Island enjoyed a prosperous fur trade and logging industry before becoming a gracious hostess to summer tourists. As you bike the routes described in this section, you can gain an understanding of the island's past while you enjoy the experiences of a tourist.

We have planned four routes totaling about twenty-three miles. All of the routes lead to Big Bay Island Park, a long stretch of sandy beach where you can picnic, swim, sunbathe or take a barefoot hike along the scenic shore. Route 1 is a straight stretch through the interior of the island to the beach. It is probably the route most popular with bikers. Route 2 takes you past the Indian Cemetery where Michel Cadotte is buried, along the south shore to the beach. Route 3 winds along the north shore past an impressive stand of white pine before cutting across the middle of the island enroute to the beach.

Abandoned homesteads lend interest to biking on Madeline.

Route 4 branches off Route 3. It takes you on good dirt road through remote woodland, then circles back to join Route 3 and continue to the beach. All of the roads on the island are an even grade, so you can bike effortlessly along and enjoy the scenery. Routes 1, 2 and 3 are excellent biking. All the roads on these three routes are paved except Hagen Road to the beach and a short stretch on South Shore Road. These dirt roads are usually firmly packed, however, and bike almost as easily as the paved roads.

Route 4 is nearly all on dirt roads. Although usually the dirt is firmly packed, one three-mile stretch is intermittently loose gravel and pavement. To adapt to the different surfaces you'll have to concentrate on your pedaling as you bike this road.

Although a modern marina, golf course and condominiums near La Pointe attest to Madeline Island's tourist industry, most of the island retains a wilderness setting similar to the other islands in the archipelago. You can participate in the merry bustle of La Pointe shops and cafes, then take off for some solitary biking into the island's interior. We thoroughly enjoyed biking Madeline Island and hope you'll find the routes described here interesting, too.

A cool drink at the water fountain in the "village square" is a good way to begin your tour of Madeline.

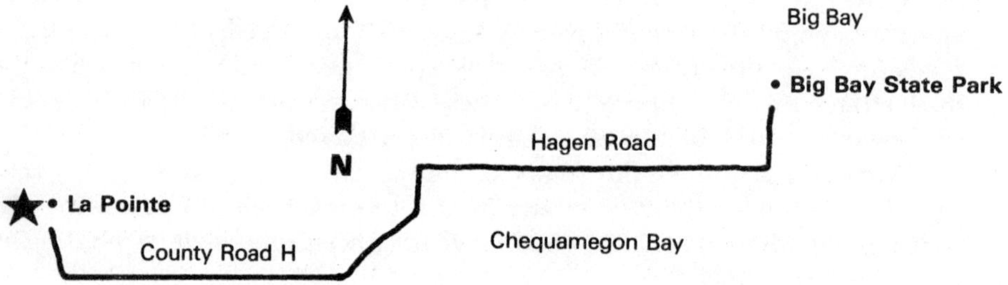

Route 1 - Big Bay Island Park

•Excellent
•One-Way
•7.3 Miles
•Even Grade
•Paved/Dirt

This tour begins at La Pointe and stretches 7.3 miles through gentle wilderness to Big Bay Island Park. On this route you'll glimpse sandy beach edging the clear blue waters of Lake Superior, a hint of the scene you'll enjoy at Big Bay. Except for Hagen Road which is firmly packed dirt, the route is paved. This is a one-way route; you must return to La Pointe on the same road or hook up with Routes 2 or 3 for more biking on the island. The entire route is also an even grade so you'll enjoy effortless pedaling to the beach.

This trip starts at La Pointe, one of Wisconsin's oldest settlements. In 1693 Pierre LaSueur, a French officer, built a fort near La Pointe and began trading with the Indians for furs. However, his trading venture was so successful that he shipped too many furs from this location. Fur prices dropped and the trading post was closed for twenty years. In 1718 the French reestablished the post and fur trading continued, first with the French, then with the British and finally with the Americans for more than one hundred years. When the fur trade waned, La Pointe became the center of the fish industry where Lake Superior catches were salted and shipped East.

Today La Pointe bustles with tourists. Several gift shops and cafes cluster near the ferry dock. A grocery store, gas station and bike rental serve summer visitors as well as the island's year-round population.

When you step off the ferry, push your bike up the brief incline and stop for a cool drink from the water fountain near the pavilion in the "village square." You'll see the museum just across the street, and you may decide to stop there before beginning your tours of the island. The Madeline Island

Historical Museum, made up of four log buildings dating from pioneer days, is located where the American Fur Company post once stood. Surrounded by a log stockade reminiscent of the early fur trading posts, the museum houses an excellent collection of Indian and early settler artifacts.

Return to the village square and head south about one block through the main part of the village. Turn left at the grocery store and bike east on County Road H. On this road you will pedal through the island's interior straight to the beach.

Before leaving La Pointe you may want to stock up on picnic supplies and stuff your swim suit into your day pack in preparation for an afternoon at the beach. Almost as quickly as you turn the corner you leave behind the hubbub of the village. Abandoned farmsteads and silent cabins mingle with the gnarled orchards and graceful birches along this route. At one point, we saw a wind generator, its blades still, reaching silently toward the cloudless sky.

But there are signs of activity along this route also. One interesting sight is the tall wire fences enclosing the islanders' gardens. Madeline Island has a large deer population partial to beans, carrots and other garden delicacies. To protect their vegetables from the deer, islanders have built high fences around their gardens. Seeing how well the plants grow within their wire boundaries, we speculated about the deer's frustration as they peer through the mesh at the tantalizing vegetables just beyond their reach.

Three miles from town we started to catch sight of Lake Superior as the road winds along Chequamegon Bay. As you ride here, you will glimpse sandy shoreline through fluttering birches and feel the cool breeze coming off the water.

A mile's pedal along the bay brings you to Hagen Road. This wide dirt road cuts through solid wilderness to Big Bay Island Park. The grade is even here and the dirt firmly packed, red clay typical of the soil found in the Apostle Islands, so maneuvering this route should not be a problem. 2.5 miles down this road turn left for an .8 mile pedal to the beach. We pushed our bikes over the long wooden footbridge leading to the beach. This bridge stretches across a wide marshy area that separates the beach from the main part of the island. Without it, the beach would be inaccessible.

Leaving the dense foliage and wooden footbridge of the marsh, we stepped onto the soft sand of the open beach. For as far as we could see in front of us, blue waters shimmered in the bright sun and the white sand waited. A few swimmers and beachcombers dotted the landscape, but finding a deserted spot was easy and we settled on a driftwood log to eat the lunch we had earned. After lunch we wandered along the quiet beach with the cold clear water of Lake Superior lapping gently around our ankles.

People unfamiliar with Lake Superior are often surprised by how cold the water is. This lake is the largest body of fresh water in the world and as you plunge in for a swim it is easy to believe the legend which says Lake Superior is the home of the gods. A place as beautiful and as foreboding as this great lake must have a special purpose.

But its special purpose for us, as we walked this peaceful shore seemed to be to loosen our muscles and lull us to quiet thoughts. On warm, sunny days few places can match the beauty of a Lake Superior shore. If the gods have a hand in that - and it's easy to imagine they do - we're grateful. The chilly water refreshed us and we were soon ready to get on the road again.

You can return on this route to La Pointe as we did, or use your map to connect along the way with one of the other routes.

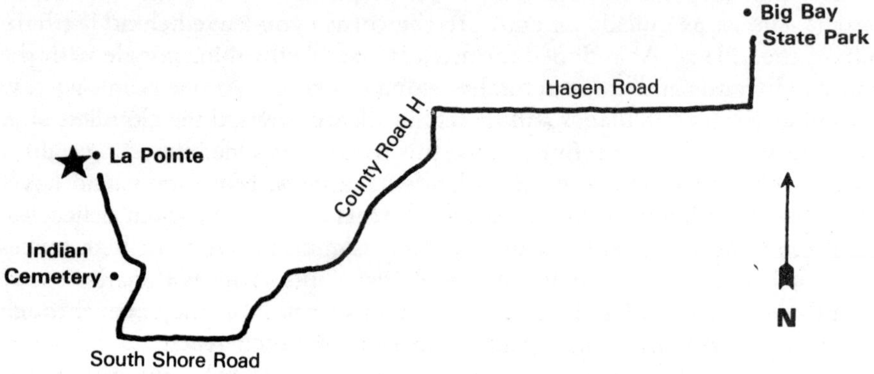

Route 2 - South Shore Road

- Very Good
- One Way
- 10.2 Miles
- Even Grade
- Paved/Dirt

This tour begins at La Pointe and winds 10.2 miles along the island's south shore. On this route you'll pass the modern marina and the historic Indian Cemetery, then continue on County Road H and Hagen Road to the beach. Except for one long, steep hill at the beginning of South Shore Road and two stretches of firmly packed dirt, one on South Shore Road and one on Hagen Road, you will bike on paved, even grades.

Beginning at La Pointe, bike south through the village toward the marina. Almost immediately you'll glimpse the tall masts of moored yachts, impatiently awaiting adventures on the lake.

The ribbon of road winds along the marina separating this watery world from the rolling green of the island's golf course. With the marina on our right and the golf course on our left, we felt a little like the pedaling of our bikes established a balance between water and land sports. Just past the marina, you'll see a sign pointing the way to the Indian Burial Ground. Turn right and wind back toward the marina. Now you are biking between the marina and the shore.

About two blocks from where you left the main road, you'll see the cemetery on your left. Park your bike near the entrance and walk into the cemetery. Tall, white stones mingle with low wooden structures to mark the graves of the settlers and Indians buried here. When the Indians converted to Christianity, they kept some of their ancient customs. One of these was the building of small houses over each Indian grave. Into this house, survivors put the dead person's personal possessions, food, water and other items needed for a comfortable trip to the next world. Although some of these houses have toppled from age, others are in remarkably good condition. Standing beside them, we found it easy to imagine the deceased on a safe journey toward heaven, and we wished them well.

Although it's difficult to read some of the markers on the settlers' graves - a few of them date back two hundred years - we did find Michel Cadotte's marker in the center of the cemetery. Influential in the community during his lifetime, he remains an important figure in death. You may want to spend a few minutes here savoring the quiet of this peaceful setting.

We have biked to this cemetery many times, but it always holds the same attraction for us. Standing beside one of the low wooden structures we listen to the gentle lapping of the lake just a few feet away and watch the cross-like shadows of the silvery masts reaching toward the ancient markers. Surprisingly the marina's activity seems to complement the cemetery's peacefulness. It helps us remember that thoughts of death need not detract from our enjoy-

Ancient wooden burial houses in the Indian Cemetery contrast with the modern marina across the street. Bikers catch a glimpse of both worlds when touring Madeline.

ment of life and that exuberant living can be a tribute to those who have died. This blending of life and death - history and present - always renews us.

When you are ready to return to your bikes, pedal back to South Shore Road and turn right. As if testing the depth of our rejuvenation, a long steep grade confronted us here. Also the road is narrow and although paved, quite rutted. Watch for cars because there is not much of a shoulder here and you will want plenty of time to adjust to any traffic. We toiled up the tree-lined road and once at the top realized that we had enjoyed the challenge.

About a mile east on South Shore Road, the route turns to the left. Here you will bike about three miles through wilderness on dirt road. The dirt is hard packed where cars travel it, but when we biked it the shoulders were quite soft; therefore, keep a sharp lookout for cars so you can steer onto the shoulder with care when needed. As we biked along this wilderness route, we caught glimpses of the lake through the trees. It is a very peaceful three miles and worth the extra concentration you may need to bike it safely.

When you reach County Road H, you can turn left and take H three miles back to town or turn right and pedal another 5.1 miles to the beach. Either way you are on the same route described in Route 1.

A long, wooden footbridge leads to the beach at Big Bay State Park.

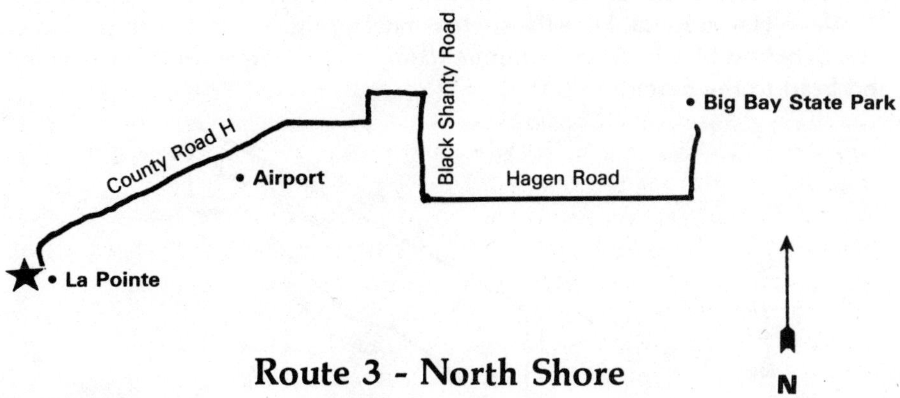

Route 3 - North Shore

•Excellent
•Round Trip
•8.7 Miles
•Even Grade
•Paved

This tour begins at La Pointe and follows the island's north shore. You will bike past a variety of landscapes until you connect with Hagen Road. From there you can either return to La Pointe (a round-trip route of 8.7 miles) or head to the beach (a one-way route of 8 miles). County Road H along the north shore, and Black Shanty Road are paved, even grades so this route is excellent biking.

Beginning in La Pointe, bike north out of town. Although houses and cottages line the road, you will find the pace slower here than on the southern route to the marina. County Road H winds past the library on the right, a lovely old building where you can sometimes buy used paperbacks for leisurely summer reading, and an old cemetery on the left where some of the island's early settlers are buried. Then before you know it, you are out of town and biking through a stately stand of tall pines. The trees have been pruned so their tall, straight trunks stretch toward the sky, feathering out finally in a dense canopy far above your head. As Kathy biked along, a deer stepped out of the woods and stood silently while Larry took its picture. The animal's apparent calm seemed appropriate in this shaded, subdued setting, and we slowed our pace a little to savor the quiet here.

Before we were ready to give up this peaceful pine forest, it ended abruptly at an open field. The sun splashed across our faces as we biked past the island's airport, a long strip of grassy field planned for small planes. Before long, however, trees grew near the road again, sheltering us from the late morning sun.

To complete this route follow County Road H 3.9 miles to Black Shanty Road, a wide, paved road cutting through the wilderness. Turn left and bike .8 mile to Hagen Road. Here the route connects with Route 1. You can either turn right and bike back to La Pointe (completing a circle route) or turn left and head to the beach.

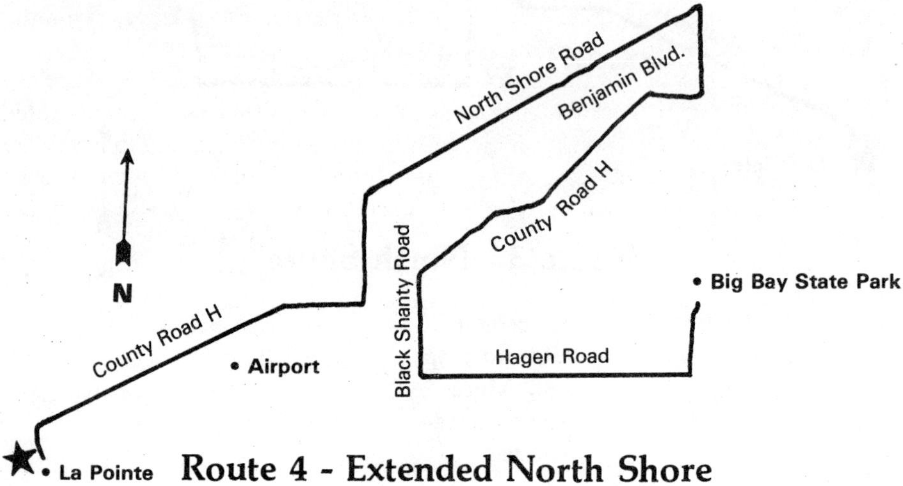

Route 4 - Extended North Shore

- •Good/Fair
- •Round Trip
- •6.3 Miles
- •Even Grade/Gradual Uphill
- •Dirt

This route extends the North Shore route. 3.4 miles from La Pointe it connects with Route 3 and circles 6.3 miles to Black Shanty Road where you can bike to the beach along roads described in Route 3. This 6.3 mile extension takes you through some of the island's most dense wilderness. Biking is good along this route, but the roads are dirt with some gradual uphill pedaling so only dedicated bikers will want to branch off from Route 3. This extension adds 5.8 miles of biking to Route 3. The total trip from La Pointe to the beach is 14.3 miles.

To start this route, bike north out of La Pointe on County Road H past the pine forest and the airport as you did in Route 3. About one-half mile past the airport, start looking for North Shore Road which cuts off to the left from County Road H.

As we turned off the main road we coasted down a slight hill and knew immediately we were biking through different landscape. Along this route slim white birches contrasting with the red-clay road seemed to stretch indefinitely. Occasionally a narrow road meandered through the trees toward a cottage hidden in the woods, but signs of human activity were definitely limited here. We did not see a car while we biked this road; instead, deer tracks crisscrossing in the soft dirt pointed our way. The steady exercise of our rhythmic pedaling relaxed us and we felt attuned to this remote area.

Three miles of solitary biking brought us to Benjamin Boulevard, a short dirt road cutting straight across the island. Here you'll see a marker commemorating T.S. Benjamin. One of the island's summer residents, Benjamin built this road that is named for him.

Turn right onto Benjamin Blvd. and pedal to County Road H. The county road is intermittently dirt and blacktop. We pedaled slowly and concentrated on our biking along this 2.7 mile route because our touring bikes were sometimes difficult to control as they went from hard surface to loose gravel. The traffic also picked up here because there are two campgrounds on this road. But we did meet a number of bikers here, so despite its disadvantages, this road is evidently popular with bikers.

When you reach Black Shanty Road, you can either take it to connect with Route 3 to the beach or stay on County Road H and return to La Pointe.

County Road H winds along Lake Superior for a beautiful biking view.

WASHINGTON ISLAND

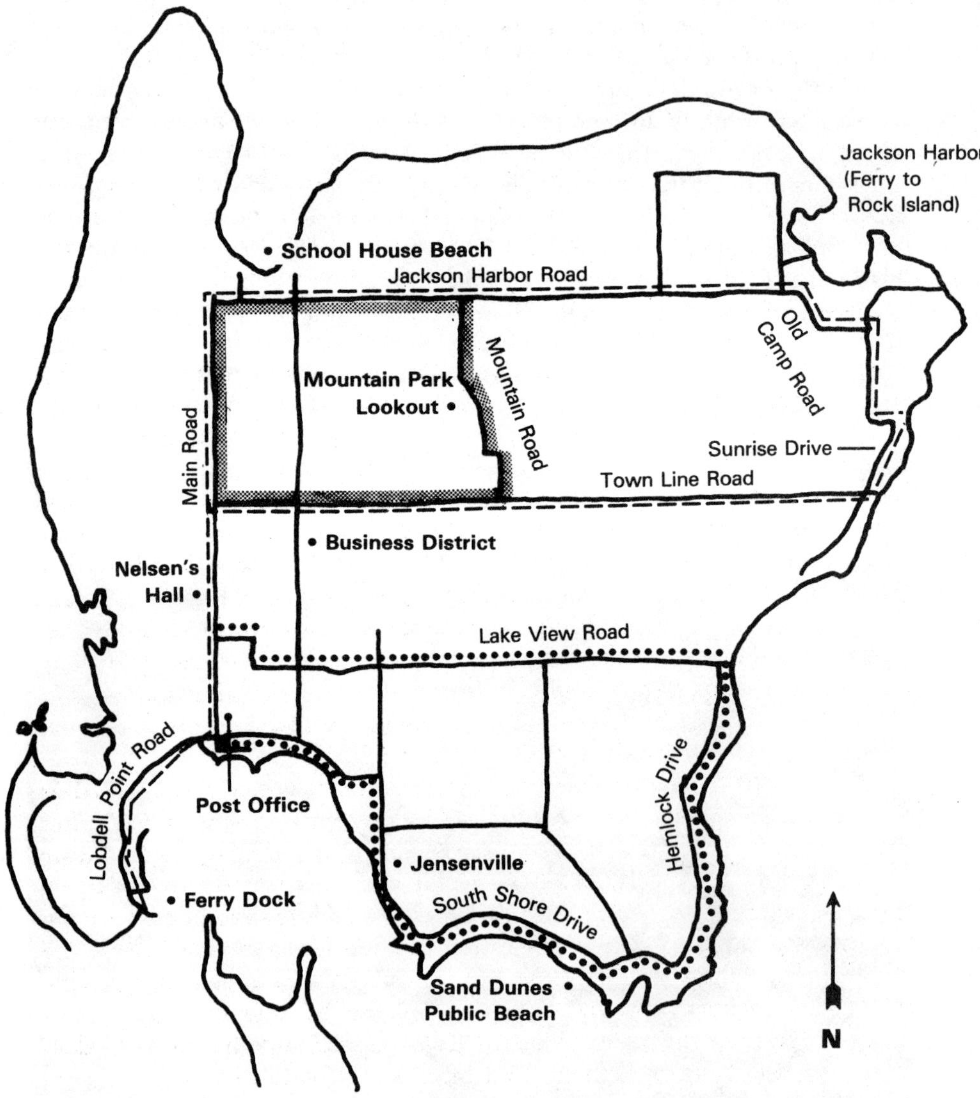

Route 1 – – – – – – – – 1-Circle Tour to Jackson Harbor
Route 2 ▒▒▒▒▒▒▒▒ 2-Circle Tour to Mountain Park Lookout
Route 3 • • • • • • • • • • 3-Southern Shore Circle Tour

Washington Island

Located in Lake Michigan just off the northern tip of Wisconsin's Door County Peninsula, Washington Island is a place of contrasts.

The temperate climate and fresh lake breezes make the island's thirty-six square miles a favorite with tourists. But the waters around Washington Island are often turbulent and have earned the passage separating the island from the peninsula the nickname Death's Door. According to popular legend the strong currents and gusting winds along this narrow passage sent many Indian canoes to the bottom. Larger vessels manned by European entrepreneurs didn't fair much better. In 1872 more than one hundred boats encountered problems while sailing across the six-mile-wide passage. Probably the most famous shipwreck on Death's Door is the Griffin. Built by French Explorer Robert La Salle, the Griffin was the first sailing vessel on the Great Lakes. Headed back to Mackinac Island with a load of furs, the Griffin sailed from Detroit Harbor on September 18, 1679. But it never reached its home port. The ship vanished, presumably while crossing the channel and no clues have ever been found to explain its disappearance. Colorful legends surrounding the Griffin disappearance add intrigue to this otherwise peaceful setting.

Washington Island, itself, is famous for more gentle reasons. A farming community, the island was originally settled by immigrants from Iceland. In 1870 thousands of Icelanders settled on Washington Island. Today the island is the oldest Icelandic settlement in the United States.

A car ferry from Northport on the Peninsula takes you to Detroit Harbor on the island. The ferry leaves every half hour from 7:45 a.m. to 6:30 p.m. during the summer months. It also runs evening trips on Friday night during peak times. The ferry costs $6.50 for a bike and rider round trip. For $5.50 more you can take your car. When we biked Washington Island we took the last Friday night ferry across Death's Door. A warm breeze ruffled the stillness of the balmy summer night, but we still felt a bit apprehensive as the large car ferry chugged slowly across the channel. Our worry was our imagination working, however. Modern Coast Guard surveillance has taken the risk - but not the excitement - out of crossing Death's Door.

Arriving safely on the island, we planned three routes totaling almost 28 miles along which you can see the tourist sights as well as the scenery for which Washington Island is famous. Route 1 takes you from Detroit Harbor around the northern half of the island. Route 2 is a round trip through the main shopping area to Mountain Park Lookout. Route 3 takes you around the

The bikes waited for us as we took a few minutes from pedaling and climbed to the top of Mountain Park Lookout.

southern end of the island past Sand Dunes Public Beach and through the wilderness along Hemlock Drive.

All of the roads on the island are an even grade and most are paved so you should find easy biking here. The wind that keeps the air pure and makes Washington Island a popular retreat for hay fever victims, also affects bikers, however; you may find yourself pedaling against the wind many places along these routes. But even considering the wind, Washington Island is a gentle place. You can easily forget the extra effort the wind makes for you while you watch the prairie flowers nodding in the breeze.

Washington Island's pleasant blend of rolling countryside and friendly wilderness make biking its roads an ever-changing adventure.

Large waves crashed against the rocky shore on School House Beach.

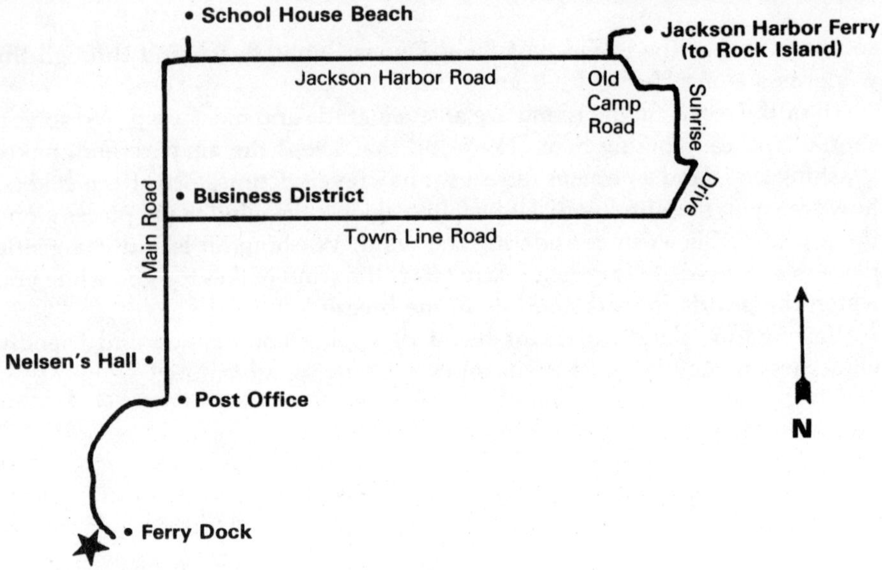

Route 1 - Circle Tour to Jackson Harbor

- Excellent
- Round Trip
- 13.2 Miles
- Even Grade
- Paved/Dirt

This route begins at the ferry dock, continues through the business district and along the northern end of the island to Jackson Harbor. From Jackson Harbor you will return, through the interior of the island, to the business district. The roads along this route are even grade and except for a couple miles along the eastern shore they are all paved. This route, totaling 13.2 miles, is planned to include many of the most interesting sights on the island. We met a number of bikers along this route and it seems to be an especially popular road on the island.

Begin this circle tour at the ferry dock. The road leading to the business district is tree-lined and paved. Wide paved shoulders make it easy to bike even when ferry traffic is heavy. It seems as though islanders have planned for bikers and are inviting them to enjoy touring Washington Island.

The gently sloping road is fast biking and we had soon completed the 1.6 miles to the post office. Here a grocery store, hamburger stand and motel cluster around four corners. Turn left and bike toward the main business district. Here the paved, even grade makes biking easy. This is one of the most populated paths of the island, so we biked past a school, stores and houses. One of the most interesting places was Nelsen's Hall, a low, wooden building on the left. Built in 1899, Nelsen's Hall is the oldest meeting place on the island. The first owner Ted Nelsen made his own ice cream and beer behind the inn. Today, as a bar and pizza place, it continues to be a place where people congregate and rest from the road. Although we had not "biked up a thirst," we couldn't resist stopping for a soda in this historic place.

From Nelsen's Hall, bike straight on Main Road to Jackson Harbor Road. This pleasant 2.8 mile stretch takes you past wide meadows where delicate Queen Anne's lace and chicory, for which the area is famous, wave in the wind. When we biked this route, we pedaled against quite a strong head wind, but the meadows were so beautiful the time seemed to go fast despite the resistance.

2.8 miles from the four corners you'll come to Jackson Harbor Road. Turn right here and almost immediately you'll see a sign to School House Beach. Turn left and bike the short distance to the beach.

Long before we could see the beach we could hear the surf crashing against the rocks. But even that did not prepare us for what we saw when we parked our bikes under the evergreens bordering the beach and walked toward the water. The entire beach was covered with large white rocks, rounded into uniform shapes of about three-to-six inches in diameter by the constant surf action of the water. The sound we had heard was the surf crashing against this rocky beach. What surprised us even more was the way people were enjoying this area. All along the beach, sunbathers sat in lawn chairs facing the open lake while swimmers stood waste deep in water just off shore. Everyone waited for the next wave. As it came rolling toward shore, the swimmers rode along on the crest of the wave and everyone anticipated the loud crash and shower of "sea spray" as the surf broke against the rocks. After the quiet white sand beaches we had enjoyed on most of the island bike trips, School House Beach was a dramatic change. We lingered here, watching a wave begin far out in the open lake and gather speed as it rolled toward shore. Growing larger and larger it raced toward us, crashing finally against the rocks and sending a cool mist over our faces. Watching the waves, it was easy to believe the legend we had heard earlier about Death's Door. This water would have indeed been a challenge to navigators of small crafts.

From School House Beach return to Jackson Harbor Road and bike east 3.6 miles to Jackson Harbor. This moderately hilly road takes you past uncultivated fields and small farms to the island's fishing village. Turn left at Indian Point Road and bike .3 mile past the fishing village to Jackson Harbor. Here the ferry to Rock Island leaves hourly. A state park, this island has many attractions. The first lighthouse to operate on the Great Lakes was built here and is still in operation. A relative of Daniel Boone is buried here and the last survivor of the Boston Tea Party once lived here. There are campgrounds and hiking trails on the island. You may decide to take the ferry for a pleasant side trip to the island. You should plan to take your bike with you because there isn't any place to leave it at the harbor.

From Jackson Harbor, return to Jackson Harbor Road and turn left. Now you are biking on Old Camp Road along the eastern side of the island. This winding, gravel road cuts through the wilderness part of the island. You'll pass a few cottages here, but Wisconsin woodland predominates.

A .6 mile pedal brings you to Sunrise Drive. Turn right here and bike south through peaceful woodland. Moderate grade adds a challenge to this good gravel road. An .8 mile pedal brings you to Town Line Road. Turn right here and bike under a leafy canopy. This road cuts through the center of the island, and as you bike it, you will see a smattering of the different kinds of scenery on the island. At first a gravel road takes you through a heavily wooded area, then the gravel turns to pavement and the scenery also changes. Fields and farms line the road here. Acres of Queen Anne's lace and chicory nodded greetings to us as we biked past. After coming out of the woods the sun felt good on our faces and we smiled back at the merry-looking flowers. 4.1 miles of excellent biking brings you back to the island's business district and the end of this tour.

Queen Anne's lace nodded greetings to us as we biked Washington. At one point, the friendly flowers lured Kathy from the road for a walk through this field of flowers.

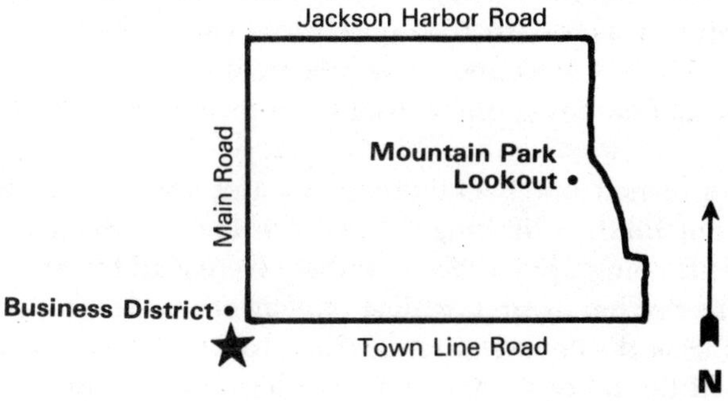

Route 2 - Circle Route to Mountain Park Lookout

- Excellent
- Round Trip
- 4.7 Miles
- Gradual Downhill/Even Grade
- Paved

Beginning at the business district, this circle route takes you to Mountain Park Lookout, then back to town on Town Line Road. The entire route is paved and if you bike the route clockwise as it is described here, it is all even grades or gradual downhill slopes. This 4.7 mile route through peaceful countryside is excellent biking and a good way to begin or end a day of traveling.

From the business district, bike north on Main Road to Jackson Harbor Road; then turn right and bike 1.5 miles to Mountain Road. These roads are described in Route 1. But when you turn right on Mountain Road you will be biking through new territory. Mountain Road, a restful, winding country road, leads to Mountain Park Lookout. From your vantage point at the top of the lookout tower, you can see for miles across this lovely island.

We parked our bikes at the foot of the "mountain" and climbed the rustic steps to the tower. The steps are rocks inset into the side of the steep hill, so it seems a little like you really are mountain climbing. At the top of the hill, we stopped to rest a minute before continuing our climb up the tower steps for a panoramic view of the island.

Finally at the top of the tower, we surveyed the island. Fields and forests stretched out in all directions with ribbons of road outlining them. But what caught our attention was a barn roof just below us. Multi-colored shingles gave the roof a patchwork look and we wondered if the owner, knowing how many people would look down on his roof from this location, had planned it that way.

Reluctantly we turned out backs on man's and nature's art works and started back to our bikes. Climbing down from the hill seemed even more challenging than climbing up had been, and we were glad to get back on our bikes. The regular rhythm of tires against pavement was reassuring. We had biked so much during the course of researching for this book that we seemed to have developed the biker's version of "sea legs." We were most comfortable biking.

From the top of Mountain Park Lookout we could see far across Washington Island. A barn roof with multi-colored shingles in a patchwork pattern caught our attention.

The .5 mile from the park to Town Line Road is an easy downhill grade. You can practically coast this distance, so sit back and enjoy the gracefully sweeping curves along this pleasant road. As you drift along, watch for bluebirds. Their houses, perched on fences, line the road here and seeing one of these vividly colored birds against the white fields of Queen Anne's lace is an added bonus to this route.

At Town Line Road turn right and bike on roads described in Route 1 the 1.8 miles to the business district.

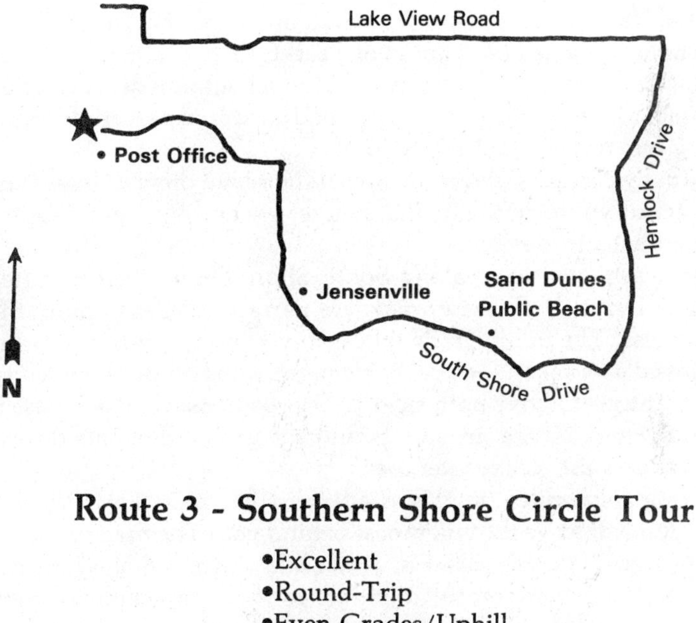

Route 3 - Southern Shore Circle Tour

- Excellent
- Round-Trip
- Even Grades/Uphill
- 9.9 Miles
- Paved/Gravel

This route takes you along the island's southern shore to Sand Dunes Public Beach, then swings north through some of the island's most attractive wilderness. The circle route is completed by a road that cuts directly across the island, linking the eastern shore with the business district. About one-half of this 9.9 mile route is paved; the rest is on good gravel roads. Although there are some uphill climbs, there is also a chance for some fast pedaling on even grades. Altogether, we think you will enjoy biking through the varied terrain on this route.

Starting at the post office we biked southeast on Detroit Harbor Road for 1.2 miles; then turned left on Rangeline Road. This paved, tree-lined route is an even grade and, anticipating lunch on the beach, we pedaled the 1.5 miles quickly. Just before the beach the road dipped toward the water and we coasted through Jensenville, a small fishing village with a marina and charter service. As we biked out of town, we could see sand dunes rising like large cushions on our right and we knew the beach was just ahead. We parked our bikes near the road and, carrying our lunch, walked the short distance over the dunes to the beach. Tall grasses, waving in the gentle wind, and colorful flowers pointed our way to the beach.

Sand Dunes Public Beach contrasts sharply with School House Beach on the opposite shore. Here the water laps lazily against the soft sand and the only sounds are the flapping of bird's wings as they circle overhead watching for a handout. Although they are very different, we enjoyed both beaches. Watching the waves crash against the rocks on School House Beach was exciting; listening to the gentle lapping of peaceful water along a sandy shore was soothing. Washington Island seemed to fit all our moods. A large Golden Retriever ambled over to share our lunch and we dozed peacefully in the sun, appreciating our respite from the road.

But eventually curiosity about the rest of the island drew us from this quiet spot. We packed up the leftovers that neither we nor our canine guest could eat and hiked back to our bikes.

From the beach, you head along South Shore Drive, then turn north to bike Hemlock Drive. Both these roads are narrow, winding routes through dense wilderness. The uphill grade will help you burn a few calories if, like us, you enjoyed a lunch on the beach. Hemlock Road takes its name from the large trees that tower above both sides of the road. As we biked these roads, the wilderness quiet settled around us and we let our thoughts drift as our bodies geared into the steady exercise.

After biking four miles on this road, turn left onto Lake View Road. Gradually, you will leave the wilderness behind you. The road turns to pavement and the trees give way to fields. As we biked here, the sunshine warmed our backs and we paid more attention to our surroundings than our thoughts.

This road is a steady uphill climb past old homesteads and uncultivated fields. At one point we biked under a leafy canopy formed by large trees bordering the road, but usually we biked under an open sky. Unlike Hemlock Road, where we had felt alone in the wilderness, this route reminded us that Washington Island is a popular tourist center. Bikers sped past us when we stopped to enjoy a hilltop view and in the distance we could see bikers criss-crossing the patchwork pattern of roads and fields. Everyone seemed to be thoroughly enjoying biking on this island.

3.2 miles on Lake View Road brings you to the business district and the end of this route.

Larry pauses to enjoy the view on Washington Island.

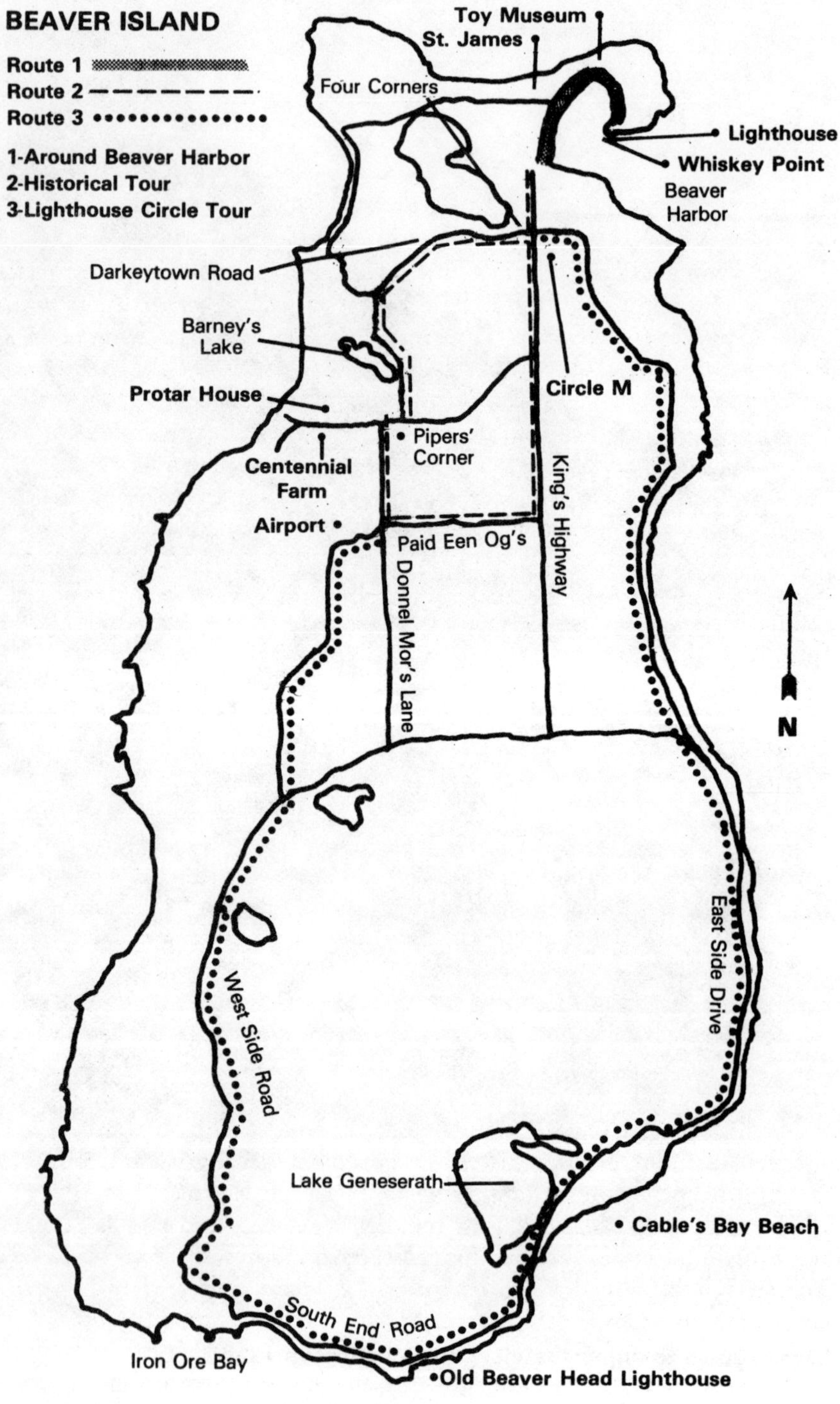
BEAVER ISLAND
Route 1
Route 2
Route 3
1-Around Beaver Harbor
2-Historical Tour
3-Lighthouse Circle Tour
Toy Museum
St. James
Four Corners
Lighthouse
Whiskey Point
Beaver Harbor
Darkeytown Road
Barney's Lake
Protar House
Circle M
Pipers' Corner
Centennial Farm
Airport
Paid Een Og's
Donnel Mor's Lane
King's Highway
N
East Side Drive
West Side Road
Lake Geneserath
Cable's Bay Beach
South End Road
Iron Ore Bay
Old Beaver Head Lighthouse

Beaver Island

Some people think it looks like a beaver. Others say it resembles an emerald sparkling in the clear blue water, but however it strikes your imagination Beaver Island is a remote island hideaway. Located in Lake Michigan thirty-two miles from Charlevoix, the island is seventy square miles of quiet roads, dense forests and long sandy beaches. St. James, the only town, nestles along peaceful Beaver Harbor where fishing boats and sailing yachts find refuge from Lake Michigan's challenging waters.

But Beaver Island was not always as idyllic as it appears today. As the site of the only monarchy ever established within the boundaries of the United States, this quiet island harbors a tumultuous past. In 1848 James Jesse Strang, self-declared successor to Mormon leader Joseph Smith, led his followers from Wisconsin to Beaver Island. Here, free from intervention by the more traditional Mormons led by Brigham Young, Strang and his followers built roads and established farms. Eventually, they excluded many of the island's first settlers and began to consider Beaver Island their special kingdom. Strang, a controversial figure who served on the Michigan State Legislature, had himself crowned king of Beaver Island in 1850.

But tensions grew, both within the Mormon community and from outsiders to the kingdom and in 1856 Strang was fatally wounded as he stepped onto a boat. After his death many non-Mormons who had been excluded from the island during Strang's reign returned to Beaver Island and forced the leaderless Mormons from the island. Although the Mormons never returned to Beaver, many of their roads, cleared fields and log houses remain as a memory of the time they spent here.

After Strang's followers left, Irish fishermen gradually settled the island. They developed the fishing industry and dubbed their new homeland "Emerald Island" because it reminded them of the lush green land they had left behind. Today Beaver Island glistens in Lake Michigan's icy blue waters. A special blend of exciting history and peaceful present, it attracts sportsmen and nature enthusiasts who appreciate its special charms.

Part of the island's appeal is its remoteness. A two-and-one-half hour ferry ride from Charlevoix, a bustling resort town, is necessary to reach Beaver. The ferry leaves once a day (twice on weekends during the summer), and costs $24, round trip for a bike and rider. Cars are an additional $40.

Waiting to board the ferry, we were caught up in the bustle of activity on the dock. Groceries and other necessities were skidded on board to fill the

Wilderness biking is the usual experience on Beaver Island.

dark holds of the boat. Everything the islanders needed seemed to be shipped on the ferry. We even saw a centerpiece of cut flowers carefully carried aboard. Watching all this, we felt as though we were soon to board a freighter for an ocean adventure.

Our sense of isolation increased as the ferry moved out of the harbor. The draw bridge spanning Lake Charlevoix yawned open and we chugged into the open waters of Lake Michigan. For a long time, it seemed, we searched the horizon for a glimpse of land; then finally we saw the outline of Beaver Island. After the bustle on the mainland, the quiet, unhurried atmosphere of Beaver Island was even more noticeable.

Since we chose to leave our car on the mainland, we felt like pioneers with all of our gear packed on our bikes. We also enjoyed the experience of depending solely on our bikes for transportation. We biked most of the island and have plannned three routes for you totaling 46 miles. The routes vary from a 1.1 mile pedal around Beaver Harbor to a thirty-three mile tour of the island. On this island only the King's Highway and the road around the harbor are paved. So except for Route 1 and short sections of Routes 2 and 3, you will bike on dirt roads. Some of these roads are excellent for biking; others are only fair. At the beginning of each route we have carefully described the conditions of all the roads on that route so you will know what to expect and can plan your biking according to your interests and abilities. Whether you leave your car on the mainland or bring that modern transportation along as a backup, we think you will enjoy the adventure of biking Beaver Island.

A drawbridge spanning Lake Charlevoix opens to allow the ferry on its way to Beaver to pass into the open water of Lake Michigan.

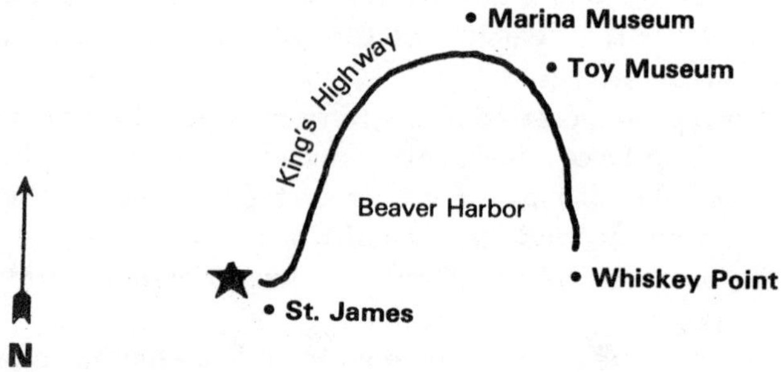

Route 1 - Around Beaver Harbor

- Good
- One-Way
- 1.1 Miles
- Even Grade
- Paved

This route takes you from the village of St. James 1.1 miles around Beaver Harbor. It is a one-way route through the island's only populated area. You will bike past museums and gift shops to a lighthouse on Whiskey Point. Although the actual ride takes about 10 minutes, you will probably want to plan a longer amount of time so you can stop at some of the interesting places along the way. The route is a paved, even grade, but the road is narrow and bumpy with regular traffic flow so take care when biking here.

This route begins in St. James, the island's only town. Here you'll find two grocery stores, a bike rental and a couple of restaurants, motels and gift shops. Turn right at the ferry dock and bike out of town around Beaver Harbor. Spacious yards and houses along the shore complement the rocking boats moored peacefully in the bay. You'll pass a marina, a marine museum and a store where you can buy smoked whitefish, an island delicacy. Several art galleries add a tourist-like touch to the fishing village atmosphere.

Another interesting stop is the Toy Museum about one-half mile from St. James. From the road, rocking chairs on the comfortable porch beckoned us toward the quaint old house, so we parked our bikes and climbed the steps to the museum. Once inside we stepped backward into a childhood of metal trucks and cackling chickens laying marble eggs.

In keeping with the antique displays, the museum offers toys for old-fashioned prices, and the children with you will have fun buying whistles for a nickel and small toys for twenty-five cents.

Leaving the museum with a little bag of treasures, we continued to the lighthouse. Although the lighthouse was locked, summer flowers waving in the yard invited us to linger here a while before returning to St. James along the same route.

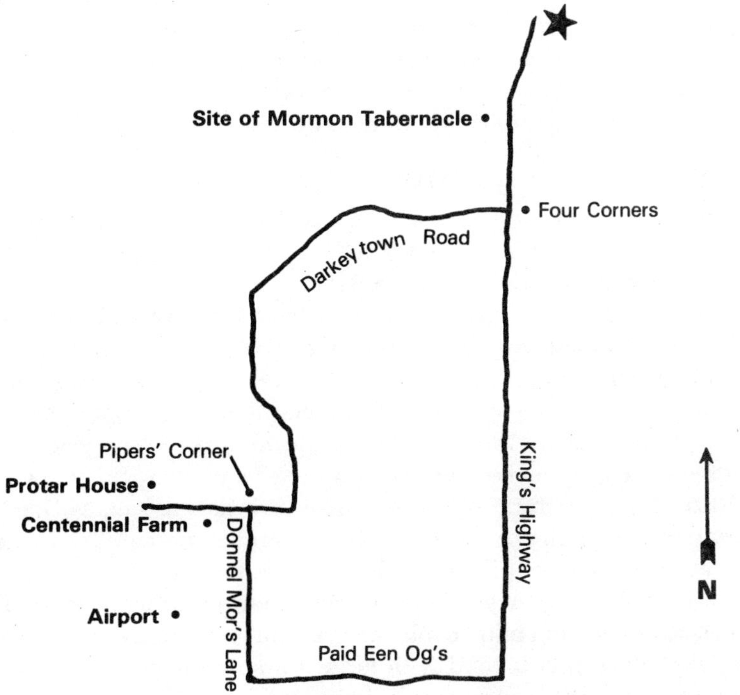

Route 2 - The Historical Tour

- Good
- Round-Trip
- 11.9 Miles
- Even Grade
- Paved/Dirt

On this route you'll bike into the island's interior past some of its most interesting historical landmarks. About five of the 11.9 miles on this route are paved. The remainder of the route is good dirt roads. You will bike on even grades past Mormon landmarks to the Protar House where one of the island's most revered residents lived; then return via a different route to St. James. Although part of the route is on King's Highway, the island's main thoroughfare, most of this route takes you through quiet countryside for a very pleasant bike trip.

Starting at the ferry dock in St. James, turn left and bike south out of town. About two blocks from the dock, you'll see a white house on the corner. This is the Mormon print shop where Strang published The Northern Islander, Northern Michigan's first newspaper. Built in 1850, it is the only building in town left standing from the Mormon era. Today it houses the island's museum with displays of Strang and Protar, two of the island's most interesting inhabitants. Although you may have just begun pedaling you will probably want to stop here because it is an excellent introduction to the places you will pass along this route. We also lingered a while on the front porch browsing through the shelves of used books before getting back on our bikes.

From the museum turn right and bike up the hill. At the top of the hill, turn left and head out of town on King's Highway. This is a gradual uphill grade on paved road. Almost immediately you'll see a resort on your left. Across from the resort is the site of Strang's tabernacle. An unobtrusive sign nearly hidden by trees marks the spot where the Mormons built their church and you might miss it unless you keep a sharp lookout.

A 1.1 mile pedal brings you to Darkytown Road. Turn right and bike on good dirt for 3.2 miles. Here you will bike beside tall cedars and spreading junipers to Barney Lake. We took this route in early evening and as we coasted down the hill to the lake we saw two fishermen trying their luck among the reeds just offshore. The popping of their fishing baits hitting water blended with the whirring of our tires over the gravel road. All of us seemed to appreciate the evening stillness of this picturesque setting.

About a mile from Barney's Lake, Darkeytown Road ends at Sloptown Road. Turn right here and bike .6 mile on good dirt road to the Protar House. This is an especially pretty road with large shade trees spreading a canopy over the road and outlining the pastures beyond. We biked past a centennial farm which has been continuously owned by the same family for one hundred years. To us, it seemed like quite an accomplishment to farm in this remote setting continuously for a century.

Just past the farm a turkey ran across the road in front of our bikes. At first we couldn't believe we had really seen a turkey running free. Attempting to explain its presence in this remote area we looked for signs of broken fences, turkey yards or a frenzied farmer following the getaway. But the farm yard was as silent as the adjoining fields. The turkey seemed in control here.

While we puzzled over the presence of the first turkey, a second one hurried across our path. Extending its long neck, it ran stiff-legged in front of our bikes before disappearing into the underbrush. We had to agree that we had just seen our first and second wild turkeys. Later we learned that wild turkeys are a fairly common sight on the island, but it seemed appropriate to us that we had seen these on our tour of the island's historical sights. They reminded us of one time when this land challenged other young adventurers and for a few minutes we felt as though we had stepped backward in time. Then a car, the only one we met on this route, sped past us, blew dust toward our bikes and interrupted our feeling of deja vu.

We stopped for a look at the Protar House where Feodor Protar, better known as the "Saint of Beaver Island" lived.

Just ahead on the right we spotted the Protar House and stopped our bikes for another glimpse into the past. The Protar House is especially interesting because it was built by Mormons and later occupied by the man still known today to islanders as the Saint of Beaver Island.

Feodor Protar, a Russian immigrant, first came to Beaver Island in 1887 when a storm caused the freighter he was sailing on to take shelter in Beaver Island's quiet harbor. He fell in love with the beautiful island and eventually retired there. He bought the old Mormon homestead and lived there for many years. An educated man, Protar gave medical care to the islanders. His services were so valuable and so respected that the islanders called him a saint and when he died they buried him in a tomb befitting that title. His old house and yard is lovingly restored and as we stepped onto the porch we almost expected Protar to open the door and ask, "Are you ill?" But only the mosquitoes greeted us and we soon mounted our bikes again to see more of the island.

From the Protar House, pedal back the way you came to Pipers' Corner. At the corner turn right on Donnel Mor's Lane and bike .5 mile. This route is also dirt and fairly easy biking on an even grade. On this road you'll pass the airport, a large field with mowed landing strips. Flying is a popular way of reaching the island, and a small plane drifted low over our heads as we pedaled along.

Just past the airport several roads angled off toward various parts of the island. Leaving the other road for another time, we chose Paid Een Og's Road, and biked 2.6 miles through unbroken wilderness. Slender white birches glimmered in the dense dark woods as we biked along. This road is a real experience in wilderness biking. Eventually, we saw a few scattered houses, then a stop sign and finally the smooth paved surface of King's Highway. "Civilization," Larry said as our tires hit pavement.

Once on the pavement the last 4.1 miles back to St. James went quickly for us. We biked past farms and corn fields on a straight, slightly downhill route right into town.

We were somewhat relieved to be back on pavement. Although the dirt roads on this route were in good condition, they were often rutted with patches of soft dirt. We did have to concentrate on maneuvering our bikes along this route, and we recommend this circle tour only to people with some biking experience. For us, the wild turkeys, peaceful lake and quiet wilderness made the extra effort to bike this route worthwhile.

One of the best things about Beaver Island is its miles of isolated beaches.

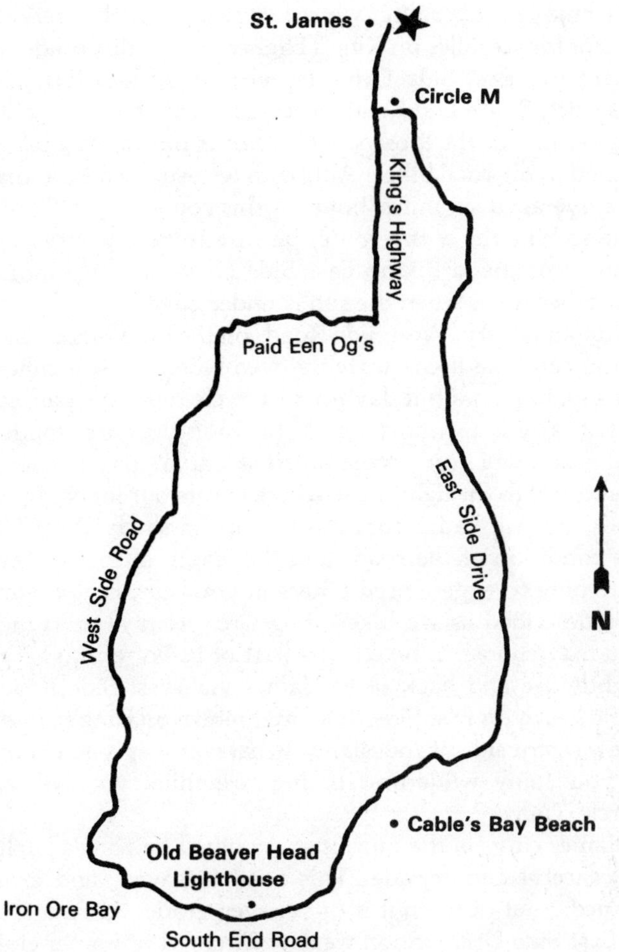

Route 3 - Lighthouse Circle Tour

- •Poor/Very Good
- •Round-Trip
- •33 Miles
- •Even Grade
- •Paved/Dirt

This circle route takes you along the island's eastern shore to Old Beaver Head Lighthouse, then back to St. James via West Side Road for thirty three miles of wilderness biking. Along this route you can stop at three beautiful beaches, climb to the top of a picturesque lighthouse and bike through unbroken wilderness. This Lighthouse Circle Tour is especially interesting for wilderness bikers.

Although we enjoyed this route, we recommend it with reservation. The entire route except for six miles on King's Highway is on dirt roads. West Side Road is excellent but East Side Drive is very rutted and difficult to bike because of loose dirt. South End Road, especially around Iron Ore Bay is also difficult biking because of the loose sand. We rode our touring bikes but this route is best suited to off-road bikes. Although we usually bike about thirteen miles/hour, we averaged six miles/hour on this route.

If you decide to bike the entire route, be sure to take plenty of food and water. We also recommend biking East Side Drive in early morning, late afternoon or at other times when the sun is under cover. In full sun you may find this road hot and dusty. West Side Road, on the other hand, is completely shaded so you can bike it comfortably even when the sun is hot.

Ideally, you should plan a full day for this circle tour. We packed a picnic lunch and started early in the morning. A thin morning haze clouded the sun while we biked East Side Drive. We stopped at Cable's Bay to cool off at the beach, then continued to the lighthouse where we ate our lunch. By that time, the sun was hot, but we had a cool return trip on shady West Side Road. Because of the condition of the roads and the length of the trip, we recommend this route only to experienced bikers in good physical condition.

This route is described as we biked it: a circle tour around most of the island. But you may choose to bike just a part of it. For example, you could bike to the lighthouse and back to St. James via West Side Road, or you could bike to the beach on East Side Road and return on King's Highway thus eliminating the western side of the island. Whatever way you choose to bike this route, if you enjoy wilderness biking, we think you will enjoy this Lighthouse Circle Tour.

Leaving St. James early in the morning, we biked on King's Highway, 1.1 mile through peaceful countryside. This road is paved, and except for a gradual uphill pedal out of town it is on an even grade. At Four Corners we turned left on East Side Drive. Soon we saw Circle M, a supper club famous for its delicious hamburgers. Although it was too early in our tour to stop, we promised ourselves that we would return when we had "earned" our dinner.

Just behind Circle M is Welke Airport, so at times there is quite a bit of activity on this road. As soon as you pass the airport, however, you can settle into a long stretch of wilderness biking.

The scenery on East Side Drive varies from low marshy areas to stands of tall cedars. On this road, we most enjoyed biking past the cedars. There, tall dense trees bordering the road seemed to seclude us from the rest of the world. We savored the intense quiet and drew deep breaths of the cedar-scented air. On this hot, muggy morning biking through the cedars refreshed us.

All too soon, we left the cedars behind, and although we continued to look for more dense stands like the one we had just passed, we did not find any.

Occasionally a few stately cedars mingled with other evergreens but that one aromatic stretch of road was unique. So take your time here, enjoying the experience as we did.

For the most part we traveled this road slowly, using our bikes' middle gears and watching for loose dirt or rain-washed ruts in the road. We also stopped often for drinks and snacks to renew our energy. One time as we stopped beside the road and dug in our packs for orange juice and grapes, an old pickup truck full of young people passed us. They were dressed in jeans and long-sleeved shirts and were evidently setting off for a day's work in the woods.

"Get a truck," they called to us merrily as they bounced past.

But we laughed our disdain. "Who would ride in a truck when they could be biking," Larry said as we mounted our bikes and continued our trek to the lighthouse.

A wooden footbridge leads the way to the beach at Cable's Bay.

11.1 miles from Four Corners a sign to the beach tempted us from the road. We turned left and pedaled .2 mile down a side road to a wooden footbridge crossing Cable's Creek. Here we parked our bikes and hiked through the woods to the beach. This is quite a long walk up hill and over sand dunes but it is well worth the exertion. As we toiled over the last rise and slid down the dune toward the beach, we were impressed by the splendor of the isolated shoreline. White sand warmed by the bright sun and cooled by the gentle lapping water stretched for as far as we could see in either direction. Although the map showed this as a public beach, we were the only people enjoying it. We felt a bit like explorers discovering uncharted territory. The sense of isolation coupled with the serenity of this sun-drenched shoreline formed a special memory. At times biking this route had seemed strenuous, but a chance to enjoy this beach made our efforts well worthwhile. One of the best things about Beaver Island we discovered on this route is its miles of isolated, beautiful beaches.

We lingered here, wading in the clear cool water and relaxing in the soft sand. Then finally, knowing we wanted to complete this route before dark, we turned away from this peaceful place and hiked back to our bikes.

Refreshed by our stay at the beach, we pedaled the remaining 4.4 miles to the lighthouse with renewed energy. Although we had enjoyed the challenges of this route, we looked forward to another well-deserved rest as we pushed our bikes up the last hill to the lighthouse. The sand-colored bricks of the lighthouse blended well with the colors on the beach and the light tower rising above the trees seemed a natural extension of the wilderness surrounding it. Although the light stopped operating in 1960 after a century of use, you can climb up inside the tower. Standing on this remote tip of the island we felt how important the light must have been as it guided ships along the coast.

Thinking of the beach again, we were drawn down a steep hill behind the lighthouse to another beautiful stretch of isolated shore. Here we dug our toes in the soft, cool sand before taking to the trail again to complete the tour.

Old Beaver Head Lighthouse marks about the halfway point of this route. From the lighthouse we continued on South Shore Road along Iron Ore Bay. This is another beautiful stretch of beach which might tempt you away again from the bike route. The road, however, is soft sand very similar to the dunes that border it, so pay attention to your biking here.

Just past Iron Ore Bay the road curves left onto West Side Road. Here we biked for about nine miles through unbroken wilderness. Huge trees spread a leafy canopy over the road, and shaded us from the afternoon sun. We especially noticed the size of the birches. Unlike the slender trees we expected to see, the birches here seemed to have the time and space to reach impressive girth. They stood in stalwart clusters on either side of the road. When we took this route, (just after a rain) the dirt surface was packed hard and the biking on this even grade was excellent. West Side Road was a real wilderness biking experience and our favorite road on Beaver Island.

After biking about an hour on this road we left the shady canopy and pedaled blinkingly into the sun. Here as roads branched off in all directions, we again chose Paid Een Og's and biked back toward St. James on roads described in Route 2. Even though we biked the same road, we made one variation in the route. Thinking we had earned a treat, we stopped in late afternoon at Circle M for one of their famous hamburgers. It was indeed delicious and we especially appreciated it after the rugged biking adventure we had just enjoyed.

A 1.1 mile pedal from Circle M took us back to St. James and a welcome rest.

Old Beaver Head Lighthouse marks the halfway point on the route around Beaver Island.

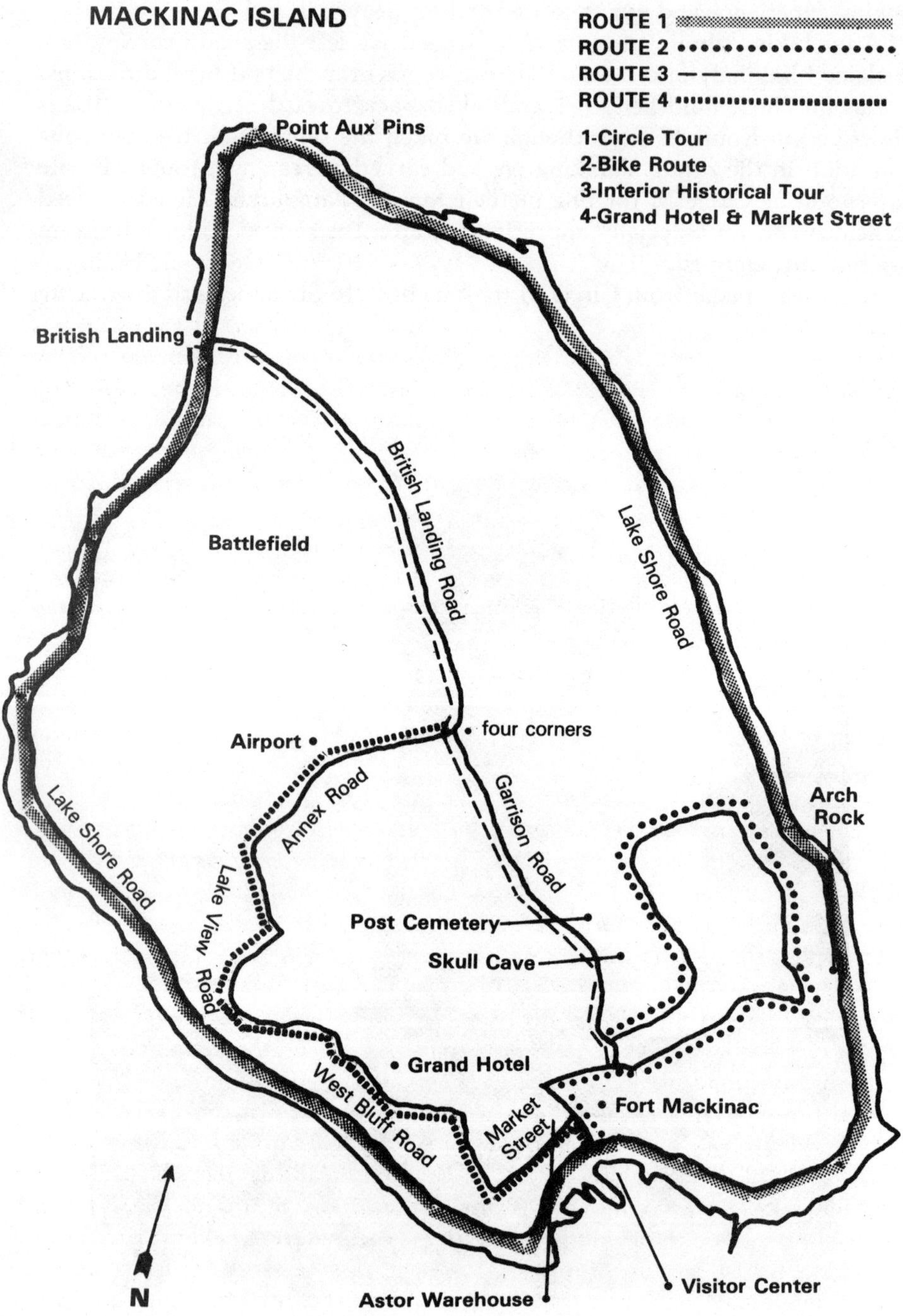
MACKINAC ISLAND
ROUTE 1
ROUTE 2
ROUTE 3
ROUTE 4
1-Circle Tour
2-Bike Route
3-Interior Historical Tour
4-Grand Hotel & Market Street
Point Aux Pins
British Landing
British Landing Road
Lake Shore Road
Battlefield
Airport
four corners
Annex Road
Garrison Road
Arch Rock
Lake Shore Road
Lake View Road
Post Cemetery
Skull Cave
Grand Hotel
Fort Mackinac
West Bluff Road
Market Street
N
Astor Warehouse
Visitor Center

Mackinac Island

Located at the Straits of Mackinac in Lake Huron, Mackinac Island is a biker's paradise. Except for one very steep hill that takes you to the starting point for two of our routes, most of the roads are even grades. Best of all, cars are not allowed on the island; you will have the kind of biking you have always dreamed of where bikes are the fastest vehicles on the road. You must, however, share these routes with hikers, horseback riders and horse-drawn carriages, so be prepared for slower traffic. Passing a horse-drawn carriage with a bike is a unique experience, and one of the special biking pleasures on this island.

A passenger ferry to the island leaves from both St. Ignace at the north end of Mackinac Bridge and Mackinac City at the south end. You can take your bike across for about $6.00 round trip or rent a bike from one of the numerous bike rentals on the island.

As well as a biker's paradise, Mackinac Island is a history buff's dream. Fort Mackinac is fully restored and maintained much as it was in the 1800's. Other historical sites are restored, well-marked and open to the public. Several of our routes are planned to take you past these historic locations where you will glimpse the island's military and fur trading past.

Mackinac Island was first designated as a military post by Lieutenant-Governor Patrick Sinclair in 1779. At that time Sinclair commanded Fort Michilimackinac, the British military post on the mainland. Sinclair thought the high bluffs overlooking the island's deep harbor made it a much safer place for a fort, so he moved his men to the island. You'll probably agree with him as you push your bike up Fort St. to South Sally Port. The view is outstanding from this 150 ft. high vantage point and you can imagine how much easier this point was to defend than the fort on the mainland.

From Mackinac Island, Sinclair could protect the British million-dollar fur trade. But Sinclair's excellent location did not remain in British hands for long. Although he had chosen well and the fort was quite impregnable, the treaty ending the Revolutionary War gave the island to the United States, and Sinclair reluctantly moved his garrison to nearby St. Joseph Island where he could continue to defend Britain's rights to the Great Lakes fur trade.

But the British never quite forgot the desirability of Mackinac Island and in 1812 they landed secretly on the western shore, surprised the American garrison and captured the fort. However, their hold on the fort was short lived; another treaty, this time ending the War of 1812, forced the British from

Mackinac is a biker's paradise. Here rows of bikes, ready for rental, await bikers as they step off the ferry.

Mackinac Island a second time. This time the commander moved his men to Drummond Island in an attempt to keep control of the fur trade.

Through all of this, Mackinac Island prospered. Millions of dollars were earned during the height of the fur trade. In fact, one of the sites on Market Street is the Astor Warehouse where beaver, otter, mink and muskrat furs were stored and readied for shipment east. In one year - 1822 - more than three-million dollars in furs were reportedly shipped from this location.

Although military and fur trading history predominate, Indian history is also evident on the island. Long before the British established a fort here, the Indians stopped on the island to gather food and bury their dead. The island's name is a shortened version of Michilimackinac meaning large turtle, and Indian legend still lingers near the unusual rock formations on the island.

To help you see both the Indian and European sites on the island, we have planned four trips totaling 15.8 miles. All of these routes start at the Visitor Center in the heart of the island's shopping district. Route 1 is a circle tour of the island; Route 2 is the island's only trail designed exclusively for bicyclists; Route 3 cuts across the interior of the island to the site of the British surprise landing in 1812; and Route 4 takes you past the island's famous Grand Hotel to Market Street, the historic center of Mackinac's fur trade.

All of these routes are excellent biking. The roads are paved and consistently even grade. Although the longest route is only 8.2 and experienced bikers can complete it in less than an hour, all of the routes connect. You can plan your biking so you start a new trail at the end of the one you have just finished, interconnecting all the routes for a day of pleasant biking.

As you bike Mackinac Island, you are never far from refreshments and friendly faces. The routes are short enough and the biking easy enough so even young children and inexperienced bikers can enjoy biking on the island. Whatever your biking background, we think you will enjoy these routes on Mackinac Island.

Bikes are "parked" along the main street in downtown Mackinac.

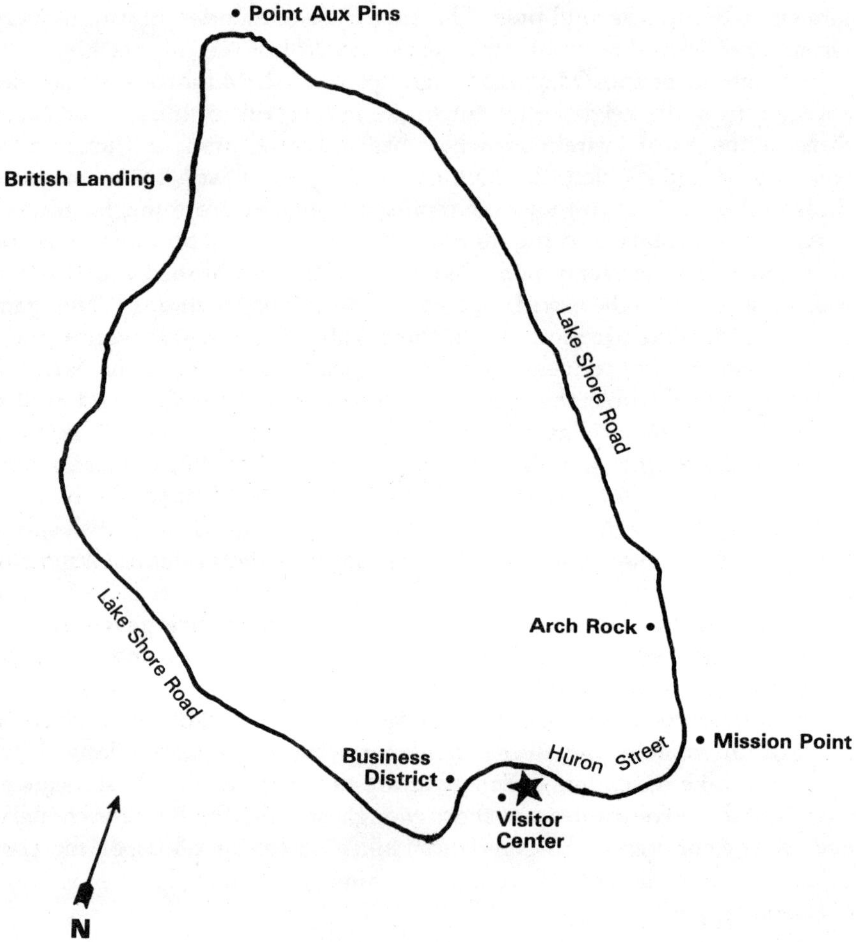

Tour 1 - Circle Tour of the Island

•Excellent
•Round-Trip
•8.2 Miles
•Even Grade
•Paved

This route takes you 8.2 miles around the entire perimeter of Mackinac Island. The paved road is an absolutely even grade along the entire route. Biking here reminded us of pedaling on a race track. If you have your own bike, you may be tempted to shift into high gear and bike this route as fast as you can. We did, in fact, bike this route two consecutive times just for the pleasure of exercising on the smooth flat track.

But several factors may keep you from going all out for the exercise. First, the scenery on this route is spectacular, so you will probably want to bike slowly enough to enjoy it. Secondly, the pedestrian traffic, leisurely hikers and horsedrawn carriages can make fast biking somewhat perilous during peak traffic times. When you take this route therefore, we suggest you relax and enjoy all the advantages of biking on this excellent road.

This route begins in downtown Mackinac Island, the heart of island activity. Fudge shops and bike rentals cluster around the ferry docks. White, horse-drawn carriages waiting for passengers line up for blocks at ferry time. Bikers drift up and down the street with total abandonment and an air of frenzied activity prevails as bikers, riders and pedestrians rush to enjoy the unique experience of "owning the road."

Caught up in the excitement, we biked down the middle of Huron Street, weaving in and out of the pedestrian traffic, dodging horses and other bikers as we picked up speed on our way out of town.

Our tour actually begins at the Visitor Center near Fort Street. From there bike east past the park where tourists lounge on the spacious green lawn and the harbor where sailing yachts rock peacefully on the gentle waters. Pedaling effortlessly, we soon pulled away from the congested downtown area and began to relax as we biked into the countryside.

As we rounded Mission Point, the sound of the lake gently washing against the shore soothed us and we began to appreciate the scenery. Here the road borders closely on the lake. White rocks jut out of the clear blue water and stretch like a gravel beach along the shore. On the inland side of the road, high cliffs tower over the trail, wedging travelers between land and water.

On the Circle Tour white rocks jut out of the clear, blue water and stretch like a gravel beach along the shore.

As you bike along, one rock formation will probably catch your attention. Arch Rock, with its bridge-like contours, stands out from the rest of the beautiful scenery. One hundred forty-six feet above us the rock stretched fifty feet across at its widest point. Wooden steps starting at the road and winding up the cliff face make the arch easier to reach now than it must have been in the past, but the impressiveness of the natural structure remains unchanged from the time when it inspired Indian legend.

Standing on the road, looking up at the rock it was easy to believe the Indian tale. According to legend, a young Indian girl fell in love with the son of the sky spirit. Because the brave was not mortal, the girl's father refused to let her marry him. The father tied his daughter to this rock where her tears washed away the center, forming the arch. Eventually, the brave found her and carried her away to his people in the sky. It's easy to believe happy endings on this island, too.

When you leave Arch Rock continue your adventure around the island. About four miles from downtown you will come to Point aux Pins, the halfway point on the tour. As you bike through a wooded area probably from where "Point of Pines" took its name, you will make the transition from the east to the west shore.

When we biked here, the east shore was sunny and a bit windy; the west shore was shady and sheltered. As soon as we rounded the point we felt like we were biking in a different place. The road was still excellent, but the landscape was more wooded on the west shore and seemed more gentle.

From Point aux Pins we began catching glimpses of the Mackinac Bridge. Viewing this impressive technological feat while we biked on a carless island gave us a strange feeling akin to deja vu.

Just past Point aux Pins you will come to a point marked British Landing. Here the British made their surprise landing and march during the War of 1812. Today there are restrooms and a refreshment stand at this point.

For us, the rest of the route went quickly. Our bikes seemed to race ahead with minds of their own. We thought how nice it would be to live on the island and start or end each day with this bike trip.

Soon we caught a glimpse of the boardwalk along the lake shore leading into town. The lilac trees nodded their greetings as we neared the business district again. Larry looked at his watch, "Let's bike it again," he said, "we have time." And without further discussion we were off through town and into the countryside for another whirl around the island.

Arch Rock with its bridge-like contours stood out from the rest of the beautiful scenery on the Circle Tour.

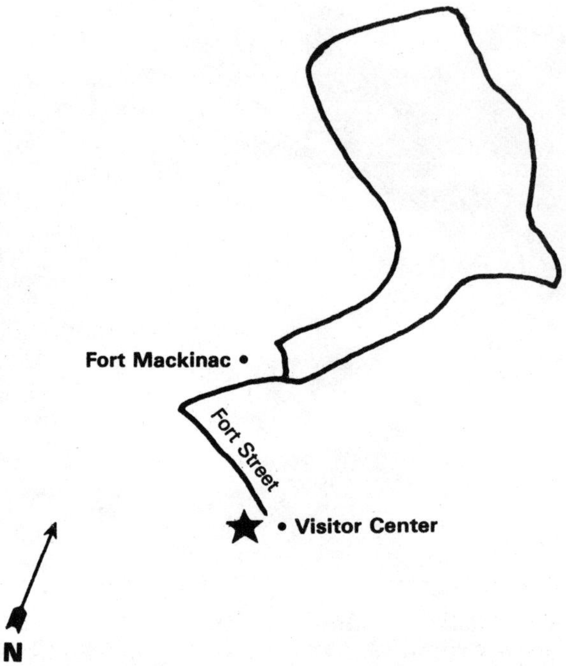

Route 2 - The Bike Route

- •Excellent
- •Round-Trip
- •2.5 Miles
- •Hilly
- •Paved

Although all of Mackinac Island is accessible by bike, only one trail is set aside specifically for bikers. This 2.5 mile path begins near the Fort and cuts through a heavily wooded area on the eastern side of the island. The narrow trail is hillier than many other routes on the island, but it is paved and excellent biking. Especially if you have just biked some of the other routes and found them congested with carriages and pedestrians, you might find this "bikers only" route a welcome change.

Beginning at the Visitor Center, you head north on Fort St. up a steep hill. As we pushed our bikes up this sharp incline toward the fort, we understood why this hilltop had been such a coveted sight for a fortress. Even today, it seemed inaccessible to us.

At the top of the hill, turn right onto Huron Road and follow that past the fort's entrance. If you are as interested in sightseeing as in biking, you should stop for a tour of the fort. You can watch soldiers in 19th century uniforms drilling on the parade grounds and shooting their muskets and cannons much as their counterparts must have done a hundred years ago. The fort, including blockhouse, commissary and barracks has been faithfully restored and is an excellent glimpse of the center of island activity in the 1800's. Imagining yourself part of the past is easy as you walk around inside this impressive fortress. We enjoyed our tour of the fort, but as we mounted our bikes for the rest of our tour, we were happy to be part of the modern age.

Just past the fort, the road forks; Garrison Road goes to the left and Arch Rock Road winds right. Straight ahead of you as you hover at the fork wondering which way to go, you'll see a sign "Bikers Only." The bike route begins here just across the street from the Boy Scout Barracks.

Eagerly we turned off the main road onto the narrow blacktopped bike path. The lane is wide enough for two bikers but a faint red line down the center indicates you should ride single file and be prepared for two-way traffic. For a short way, the bike path parallels the main road. We could hear the horse-drawn wagons clattering slowly along and we were happy to be speeding past them on our own trail.

Then the path veers away from the main road and winds through heavily wooded wilderness. We took this route in June and we were excited to find clumps of yellow lady slippers glistening in the dark woods. A rare sight in most places, they seemed to flourish along this trail.

The lady slippers were beautiful and the stands of trees impressive but most of all we noticed the quiet. We were only minutes away from downtown and the fort's activities, but we felt completely cut off from the world. This route is a real wilderness biking experience in the middle of an active tourist setting. Surprisingly, although this is designated a bike path, we did not meet any other bikers on this route. The path is hilly and secluded compared to other routes on the island and perhaps includes fewer points of interest. But it is a refreshing change from the faster pace of other areas, and we found the sight of yellow lady slippers growing profusely on either side of the path one of the most interesting things on the island. If you like biking through wilderness, this trail should interest you.

At the end of the bike trail you can turn right on Garrison Road and pick up Route 3, or you can turn left and bike back to town. We biked back to town after this route. As we headed for the steep hill near the fort, we felt smug. Now we would have our reward for the tough climb we had taken at the start of this tour. But we were surprised; going down seemed more difficult than going up had been. We dragged the textured soles of our biking shoes along the pavement as our bikes lurched ahead like eager horses. At the bottom of the hill we drew deep breaths while we grew used to a new feeling as bikers: we were more relieved to have reached the bottom of a hill than we had been to reach the top.

Perhaps you will think that in the re-telling of this adventure the steepness of this hill has grown a little and maybe you are right. But we are sure you will find the hill a challenge and, like we did, an exciting memory of biking Mackinac Island.

Bikers have Mackinac's bike route all to themselves.

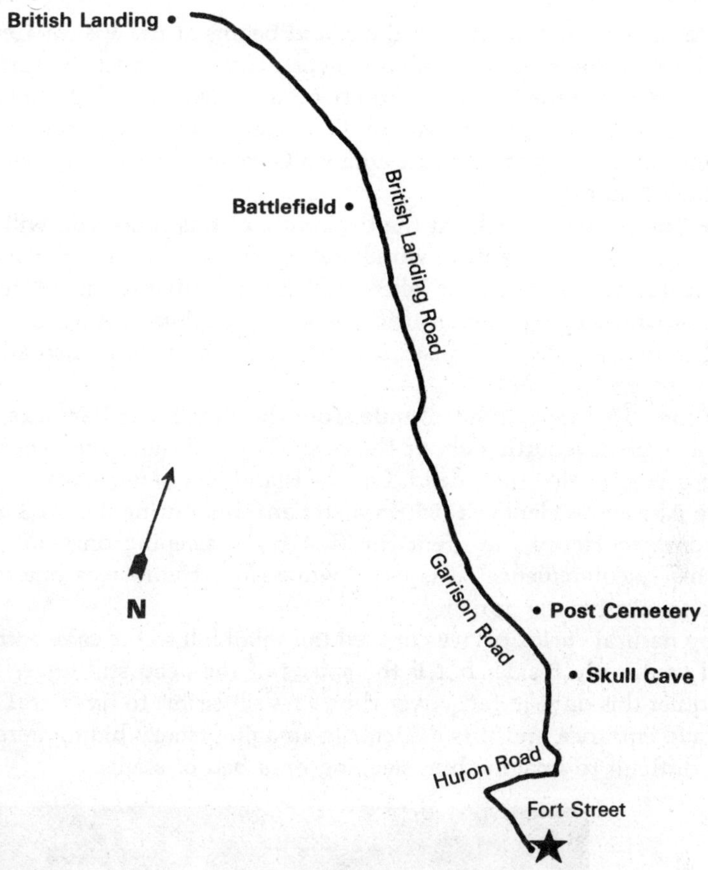

Route 3 - Interior Historical Tour

- Excellent
- One-Way
- 2.8 Miles
- Moderate Grades/Downhill
- Paved

Route 3 takes you over one of the most famous roads on the island. Cutting directly through the island's interior, this route is the one the British used when they made their surprise attack on the Americans in 1812. We'll be taking the 2.8 mile route in reverse from the way the British marched it, however. We'll start at the fort and bike to the beach where the British first landed. This paved road through the woods is excellent biking. Although you'll pedal up some moderate grades in the beginning, the second half of the route is almost all downhill. You can practically sit back and coast to the beach.

This route through the interior of the island begins at the Visitor Center. Push your bike up the steep hill on Fort Street, turn right past the fort and take Garrison Road to the left. Now you're on a straight stretch 2.2 miles to the beach on the other side of the island. (You can also pick this route up as you complete Route 2. The bike route ends on Garrison Road; turn right and you are biking Route 3.)

From the Boy Scout Barracks at the beginning of this route you will bike for several miles through beautiful woodland. Although the scenery may not be as spectacular here as along the lake shore, it is equally exciting. After the hubbub of downtown and the "traffic" on the lake shore route, Garrison Road is refreshingly quiet. The historical sights along the way also add interest to this route.

Just past the rifle range about .3 mile from the Boy Scout Barracks, you will notice a small cave jutting above the trees. This is Skull Cave, where the Indians reportedly buried their dead. On the island it is better known as the place where Alexander Henry, a British merchant, hid during the 1763 uprising. According to Henry, he spent the first night sleeping on skulls, but evidently this "inconvenience" was worthwhile since Henry was one of the few settlers to survive the uprising.

Drawn by natural curiosity, we climbed the small hill to the cave entrance and peered cautiously inside; but if the spirits of the dead still linger here, they were quiet this day. In fact, over the years silt seems to have gradually filled the cave entrance and it is difficult to imagine Henry hiding here and even more difficult to imagine him sleeping on a bed of skulls.

Larry takes a look at Skull Cave, one of the attractions of this historical tour.

When you leave the cave, continue on Garrison Road past three cemeteries, Catholic, Protestant and military. European and American settlers have followed the Indian tradition of burying their dead in this area. As we biked past the Post Cemetery, girl scouts were raising the flag ceremoniously over the graves. Here those who have died while on duty at the fort are buried. Many of the graves are not identified, but white crosses, lined up in military precision, mark the graves.

Biking effortlessly, we daydreamed along this wooded route until the "clip-clop" of horses' hooves alerted us to traffic on the road. Then we steered our bikes along the far edge of the narrow road to give the horses room to pass. Coasting within inches of a horse-drawn carriage was a little unnerving at first, but we soon became used to it. The horses didn't seem to notice us at all.

Just past Annex Road, Garrison Road becomes British Landing Road, named for the beach at the end of the road where the British landed in 1812. Intending to surprise the Americans and regain the fort, they marched up this road and successfully defeated the Americans.

Kathy checks the marker of the famous British-American battle on British Landing Road.

Two years later, the ousted Americans landed on the same beach, as the aggressor this time, and met the British in battle on a wide field near the road. You'll see a marker on your right indicating where the battle occurred. We stopped here to read the description printed on the marker. But in the silence of this warm, sunny afternoon we had difficulty picturing cannon fire.

Adding to the peacefulness of the setting is the golf course that has taken over part of the field. This is the oldest golf course in Michigan. Noting that the country club was open to the public we stopped for a soda and a chance to enjoy the lush green lawns spreading over the battlefield site. As we enjoyed the quiet summer afternoon, it seemed to us that a golf course was more appropriate to this peaceful field than a battle would have been.

When you leave the club, you can coast the short distance to British Landing. Here you may want to stop for a walk along the beach. As we walked here, we were impressed again by the changes that have occurred on this island. A refreshment stand serves festive tourists on the spot where soldiers prepared for battle. We felt happy Mackinac Island had survived such turmoil to become the relaxed, friendly place we had seen as we biked its roads.

From here you can either return to town on Lake Shore Road (described in Route 1) or return the same way you came on British Landing Road. If you return the way you came, you can pick up Route 4 at Annex Road about 1.3 miles from the beach.

Cannon marks British Landing at the end of Historical Route.

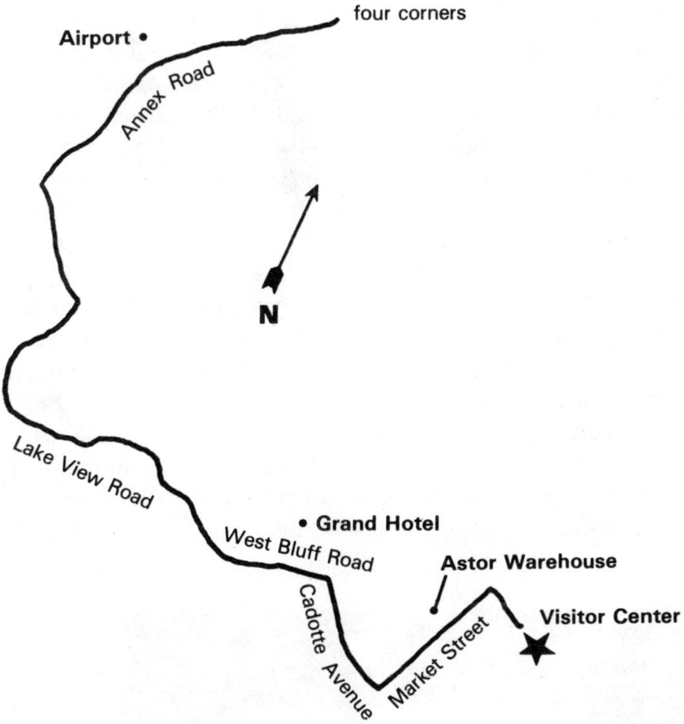

Route 4 - The Grand Hotel and Market Street

- Excellent
- One-Way
- 2.3 Mile
- Even/Downhill
- Paved

Route 4 begins at the four corners on Garrison Road. Rather than heading straight on Landing Road, turn left on Annex Road. This wooded route will take you from a wilderness setting to the center of tourist activity. The paved road is a gradual downhill grade until you near town. Then you can coast down a steep hill, past the Grand Hotel and right into the main stream of traffic on Market Street. We took this route as a branch off Route 3 making a circle route of part of Route 3 and all of Route 4. But a look at the map will show you how to combine this and other routes in a variety of ways.

At four corners on Garrison Road, turn left on Annex Road. Soon you'll see a fork in the road; keep to the right and bike past the island's airport. Daydreaming along this route was easy. As we biked through the quiet woodland, the only traffic we met was a service wagon drawn by two horses.

All too soon it seemed, we saw people milling around ahead of us, and we knew we were coming out of the wilderness and into the town again. We turned left and all of a sudden we were weaving in and out of traffic again as we sped downhill toward town. A sign on our right telling "reckless riders" to be careful both amused and cautioned us. It was the first traffic sign we had ever seen directed to speeding on bikes and horses. But coasting down this hill is probably as close as a biker ever comes to flying. Enjoy yourself, but heed the sign and use your brake as needed to maintain a reasonable speed.

This is a very busy hill because it runs past the Grand Hotel, one of Mackinac Island's most famous landmarks. Dating from 1887 this hotel is as much a favorite with tourists today as it was nearly 100 years ago. If you don't mind interrupting your coast down the hill, you can stop for a look at the impressive building and elaborate grounds. You can have lunch there or buy a ticket for a tour of the entire facility.

Bikers pause a minute to look at the Grand Hotel.

The headquarters for John Jacob Astor's fur trade is one of the historical sights on Market Street.

At the bottom of the hill, the road runs into Market Street. Historically, this was the center of the island's fur industry. Today you can stop for a tour of the warehouse from where John Jacob Astor conducted his lucrative fur trade. Here the furs were sorted and stored until they could be shipped to European and Asian markets. Gift shops and restaurants add a festive touch to this short, historical street. After the quiet on Annex Road, you may need a few minutes to adjust to the bustle again. But a festive mood prevails and you'll soon be caught up in the excitement of other carefree bikers enjoying the sights on Market Street.

DRUMMOND ISLAND

Route 1 ▒▒▒▒▒▒	1-Circle Tour
Route 2 ••••••••••••	2-Big Shoal Bay Beach
Route 3 ┅┅┅┅┅┅	3-Waterfowl Nesting Site
Route 4 — — — — — —	4-Quarry Route

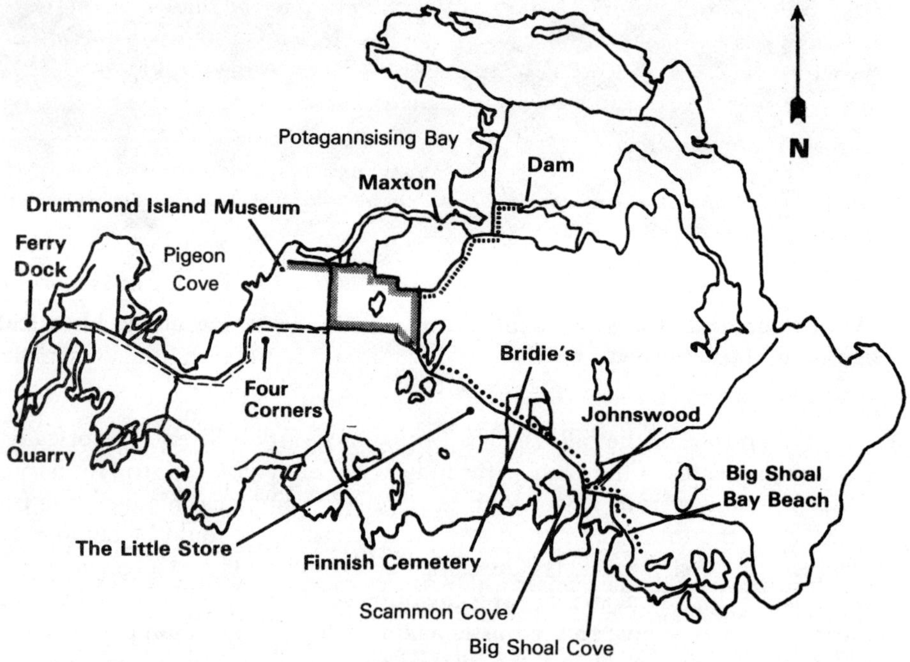

Drummond Island

Located in Lake Huron just off the eastern-most tip of Michigan's Upper Peninsula, Drummond Island has more than one hundred fifty miles of shoreline and 87,000 acres of forestland. It is the largest United States-owned island in the Great Lakes.

To reach Drummond Island, take I-75 north from the Mackinac Bridge 15 miles; then turn east on M-134 and travel 40 miles to the village of DeTour. You can also reach DeTour from Sault Ste. Marie. Travel south on I-75 about 60 miles; then take M-134 east 40 miles to DeTour. A fifteen minute ride by car ferry from DeTour takes you to the island from April to December. The ferry runs hourly, more often during busy times, and costs about $8.00 for a car and two people. Although the actual trip across the lake is short, the ferry carries only about a dozen cars at one time, so you may have to wait through several crossings before it can take you to the island.

Drummond Island is named for Fort Drummond, the last British stronghold in United States territory. A treaty signed during the War of 1812 forced the British to evacuate their fort on Mackinac Island. As an alternative, they set up a military post on Drummond Island because it was close to the Straits of Mackinac where the Indians came each year to trade furs. From Fort Drummond, the British could maintain control of the Great Lakes fur trade. But in 1828, six years after Drummond Island became part of the United States, the fur trade was waning and the British also abandoned Fort Drummond. Today quarrying for dolomite has replaced trading for furs, and only one smoke stack from the fort stands as a reminder of the past. The old British fort is now the location for one of the largest dolomite quarries on the Great Lakes and most of the fort has been excavated for this.

But the noise and dust of the quarrying is confined to one fairly isolated location near the ferry dock; most of Drummond Island is quiet wilderness. Fifty percent of the island's forestland is state-owned and many of the roads that criss-cross the area are jeep trails, therefore accessible to bikers only on off-road bikes. In planning our bike route here, we have kept to the paved roads on the western half of the island.

Starting from Four Corners, the island's only shopping center, these routes will take you through quiet countryside to points of interest on the island. We have planned four routes on Drummond Island totaling about twenty-four miles. If you look at the map you can see that we have taken one circle route through the interior of the island. The other three routes branch off

A winding, one-lane dirt trail leads to Big Shoal Bay Beach on Drummond Island.

from the circle route: Route 2 takes you to the public beach, Route 3 goes to a waterfowl nesting area, and Route 4 takes you to the quarry and fort site.

All of these routes are excellent biking. The roads are paved and winding with numerous short, semi-steep grades. We found ourselves shifting down repeatedly for these brief uphill climbs; then coasting down the other side. Larry's comment probably best sums up biking on Drummond Island: "I've never used so many of the gears on this bike," he said when we finished our last route.

But that challenge was one of the highlights of biking this island. Matching the gear to the grade added interest to the routes. Other high points of these routes were the plant and animal life we saw along the way. Yellow lady slippers, rare along most midwestern roads, grew as profusely as dandelions on these routes, and deer and ravens peered curiously at us as we sped along.

The roads are wide enough to accommodate both bikes and cars adequately, but we met very few cars on these routes. Usually we had the roads to ourselves; so we drifted along, lulled into quiet daydreams by the rhythmic whirring of our sleek, silver bikes.

We heartily recommend biking on Drummond Island; it was one of our favorite adventures. We hope you will find the routes we describe exciting, too.

A butterfly enjoys the deserted beach at Big Shoal Bay.

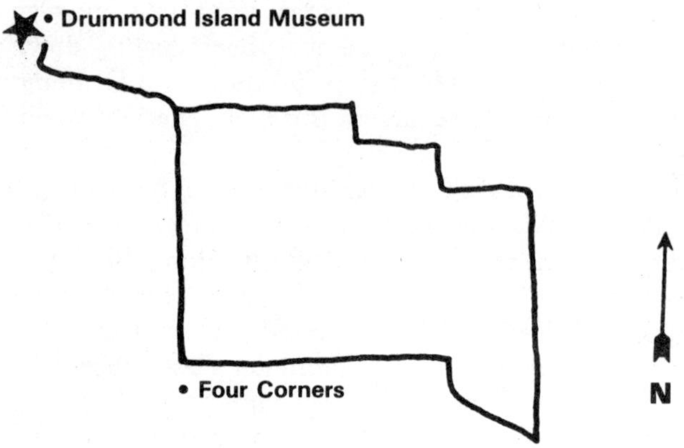

Route 1 - Circle Tour

- •Excellent
- •Round-Trip
- •7.9 Miles
- •Moderate/Even Grade
- •Paved

The Circle Tour begins at Four Corners and winds eight miles through quiet countryside. On this route you will bike through state forest land to the island's museum; then back to Four Corners. All the roads are paved; there are a few short, moderately steep grades at the beginning of the route.

Start this tour at Four Corners, the island's only village. Here you can stock up on picnic supplies at the grocery store or eat at the hamburger stand or restaurant before setting out. The restaurant serves very good white fish, a local treat. The village also includes a clothing store well stocked with sweat-shirts and other outdoor clothing and a hardware store with a good selection of bike repair materials. A gift shop, gas station and laundry complete the village.

From Four Corners bike east. A slight uphill grade with some short, moderately steep inclines takes you quickly from the activity of the island's settlement into the quiet countryside.

2.2 miles from the village turn north and pedal on an even grade through mostly wooded countryside. Follow this road for 1.6 miles, then turn west and bike through state forest land. This is the prettiest road on the route.

Here, sheltered from the wind, you can drift along under a tree canopy as the road winds gently between the towering trees.

2.4 miles along this road brings you to a stop sign and the settlement area again. To reach the Drummond Island Museum, bike .2 mile from the stop sign. Turn right, bike one block, then turn left. The museum is about two blocks down this road on the left.

The museum is located near the homestead of Betsy and Daniel Seaman, Mormons who came to the island in 1853. The first white woman to settle here, Betsy is one of the island's legends. After her husband's death, she raised eleven children on this unsettled island and managed to give them not only food and shelter but an education as well. According to island history, she taught them reading, writing and the manners she valued. Betsy was evidently as successful as legend remembers her because today there's evidence that people here still enjoy reading. The island has a small but well-stocked library open to islanders and travelers alike.

The museum itself houses a good collection of Indian and settler artifacts. Woven Indian baskets, farming and logging tools and furniture from the past give visitors an idea of what early life was like on the island. Bikers will be especially interested in the wooden wheeled bike, evidently one of the first ridden on the island.

Bikers will be especially interested in the wooden wheeled bike in the Drummond Island Museum.

Across the road from the museum is the Betsy Seaman Memorial, a drinking fountain that brings spring water to thirsty travelers. It is symbolic of Betsy's hospitality to travelers and settlers who came to Drummond Island during its settlement years. We rested here for awhile, shaded from the sun, drinking from the cool spring and looking toward the shimmering blue water of Potagannissing Bay. It was easy to imagine the first settlers sitting on Betsy's porch, drinking water from this same spring. They must have found the island as beautiful and, thanks to Betsy, as friendly as we did. But we didn't envy them. We prefer water fountains to dippers and modern touring bikes to their wooden forerunners. The island, however, still holds plenty of adventure for those who seek it along its biking trails.

Leaving the museum, return to the main route and bike south 1.5 miles to Four Corners. This is the busiest road on the route. It connects Four Corners with the island's main resort area as well as the school, library and airport. This straight road with moderate uphill grade will take you quickly to Four Corners and the end of your route.

Bikers take a drink from the Betsy Seaman Memorial fountain on Drummond.

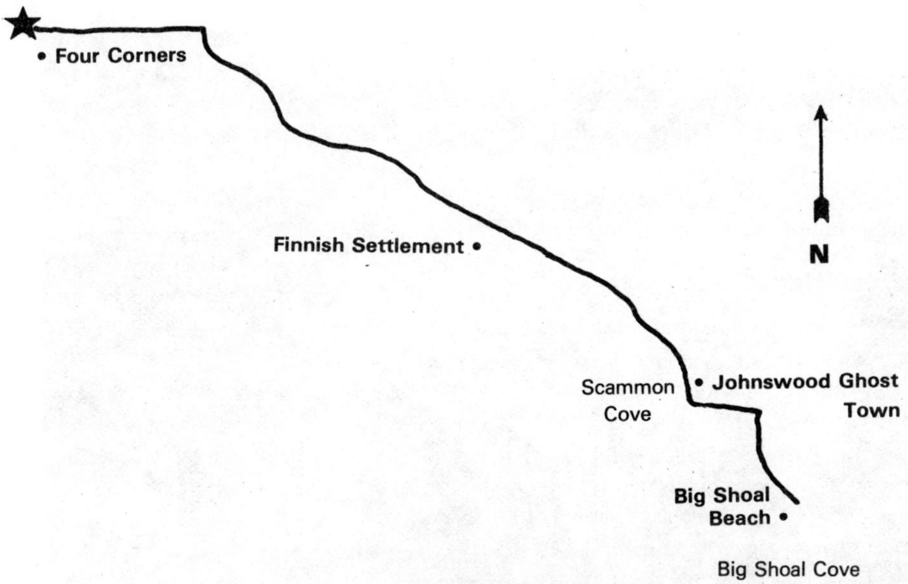

Route 2 - Big Shoal Bay Beach

- Excellent
- One-Way
- 8 Miles
- Moderate Grade
- Paved/Dirt

The Beach Route begins 2.2 miles east of Four Corners where it branches off the Circle Route. This tour takes you through a Finnish settlement and past the ruins of a logging camp to a beautiful sand beach at Big Shoal Cove. The road is paved to the beach turn-off; then dirt for .8 mile to the beach. The paved road is predominantly a gradual uphill climb to the beach turn-off with several short moderately steep grades along the way. The dirt road to the beach is an even grade. This is a one-way route; you must return on the same road to where you left the Circle Route; then either complete the Circle Route or return to Four Corners.

With a picnic lunch anchored firmly on the back of Kathy's bike we headed east 2.2 miles to a fork in the road. This time, anticipating the sandy beach at Big Shoal Cove, we chose to angle right.

For five miles we biked through the quiet countryside, marveling at the yellow lady slippers creeping from the woods to carpet the ditches along our route. At first we called to each other each time we spied one, but soon they blended with the blue-eyed grass and Indian paint brush to make a merry whirl of color as we sped along.

Quiet countryside stretches along the road to Big Shoal Bay Beach.

But the flowers were only one of several high points on this trip, and the variety of sights along the way made this our favorite route on Drummond Island.

Soon after we left the Circle Route, we rounded a bend and glimpsed a deer and her fawn standing in the overgrown field. Larry said later, he thought they were plaster-cast ornaments, so perfectly they seemed to be placed against the evergreens.

A flick of the mother's tail broke the mural-like setting and Larry reached quickly for his camera. The mother deer waited, not greatly alarmed, until she heard the snaps give way as Larry opened his camera case. Then before he could take the picture, she tossed her beautiful rust-colored head and bounded gracefully away, as her fawn followed with mirror-like leaps. The image remains a picture in our minds; but sometimes those are the best kind. We hope you, too, will collect a few of those special, private images as you bike these routes.

Along this route you will see several old homesteads; their weathered buildings and overgrown fields are merely a memory now of the hopes and dreams of those who first settled here. The homesteads are part of a Finnish settlement established in 1905 by Maggie Walz. This energetic entrepreneur thought Drummond Island was the most beautiful place she had ever seen, so she brought twenty-five Finns to the island to start an utopian society. Under Maggie's guidance they cleared the land and built a store and a school, but the dream floundered and Maggie left the island a few years later.

Today an overgrown cemetery and rock piles bordering the small fields are left to remind us of the dedication these people had to fulfilling their dreams. You'll see the cemetery on your right and the rock borders on both sides of the road when you bike this route.

About midway to the beach you'll also come to The Little Store, one part of the Finnish settlement that continues to prosper. Now an attractive little grocery, it was once the cooperative store for Maggie's utopian society. Although today it stocks all the modern conveniences of canned and frozen foods, it retains some of its Old World charm. Here you can select potatoes and onions from wooden barrels and watch as your meat is sliced on an old-fashioned chopping block. The polished floors and neat rows of canned goods blend with antique tools and utensils decorating the store. At The Little Store you can stock up for a picnic, buy an ice-cream bar, or just chat awhile with the proprietor who enjoys sharing island history.

A short pedal from the store brings you to Bridie's, a restaurant featuring home cooking served family style. The food is good but the restaurant is appealing for another reason: it is housed in the old Finnish school. A meal at Bridie's is another glimpse into the past.

Along this route, you'll glimpse even more of the island's history at Johnswood, the site of the island's largest logging operation. Once a thriving lumbering community, Johnswood doesn't even rate a marker today. You'll have to watch carefully for it. About two miles past Bridie's the road curves around Scammon Cove. On your right, jutting into the cove you'll see the pilings from the old logging camp. Then keep a sharp lookout as you bike away from Scammon Cove. The road curves away from the cove and climbs gently upward. On your left at the top of the gradual incline you can see the foundation of the camp. It is overgrown and barely visible from the road, but if, like us, you enjoy exploring ghost towns, you might decide to stop your bike and take a closer look at the ruins. Don't be too preoccupied with ghosts, however, because this area is one of the most beautiful scenes along this route. From the gradual incline, you can look out over the shimmering water of Scammon Cove and across the green fields stretching toward the lake.

Leaving the ghosts of Johnswood behind, continue about one mile to the beach turn-off. Here you leave the paved road and venture onto a winding, one-lane dirt path through the woods. On either side of the trail, stately evergreens and dainty yellow lady slippers mingle with the flat black rock spreading across the sandy soil. This is a wild and beautiful trail, a hint of the scenery awaiting you at the beach.

Don't become too absorbed in the scenery, however, because this trail requires some maneuvering around holes. It is a twisting, bumpy road, but the dirt is packed hard so you should manage it just fine with a bit of concentration.

.8 mile along this trail brings you to the beach. We walked our bikes down the short footpath of the sandy shore. As we stepped onto the beach four ravens lifted off just in front of us. They circled low overhead, calling insistently before they flew reluctantly away. They were unhappy to be disturbed and we didn't blame them. This is a beautiful sand beach with tall evergreens growing close to the shore and black rocks jutting from the water of the secluded cove.

Stealing this wilderness from the ravens for a short time, we stretched out on the sand and listened to the silence. When we started this trip, we had not known what we would find. But this quiet, wild place was an appropriate destination for the historically interesting, naturally beautiful route.

We lingered here, eating our lunch and watching the sun cast silver shadows across the water. Then, finally, we packed the remains of our lunch away and started back the way we had come, eager to see it all again.

Wildflowers grow abundantly along these biking routes.

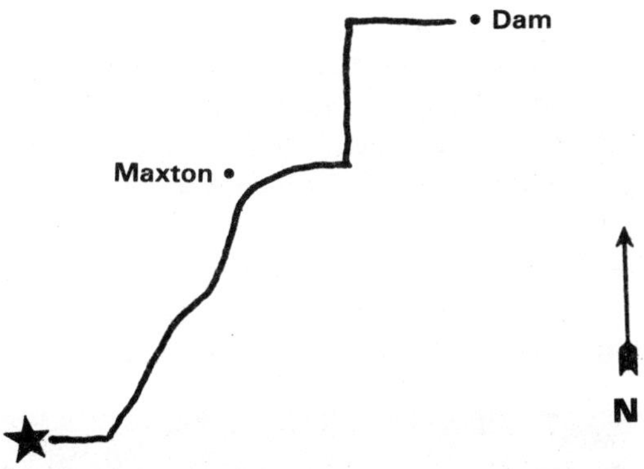

Route 3 - Waterfowl Nesting Site

- •Excellent
- •One-Way
- •3.45 Miles
- •Downhill
- •Paved/Dirt

The trip to the Waterfowl Nesting Site also branches off the Circle Route. It is a short 3.45 mile route through state forest, across Potagannissing Bay to a dam on First Lake. The paved road is gentle downhill grade. You can almost coast the entire way to the bay. But it is a one-way route. You must return on the same road to where you left the Circle Route; therefore, enjoy the easy pedaling to the bay because you will pedal steadily uphill on the return trip.

As you bike the Circle Route, rather than turning west toward the museum, head northeast to the bay. This route winds through forest land broken occasionally by a clearing for a cabin. The dense woods are a reminder of the tall timber that tempted loggers to the island. In fact, you will bike past Maxton, the site of the first big lumbermill on the island. Today you can see a reduced operation on the left, near the bay, and logging trucks enroute to the mill may pass you occasionally as you bike along.

A three mile ride brings you to Potagannissing Bay. From the bridge you can look out across the great expanse of quiet water and watch the fishermen rowing their boats slowly along the shore. The waters surrounding Drummond Island are well-known for their game fish - Walleye, Northern Pike and Bass - so you will probably see many people fishing here.

Cross the bridge, pedal up a short incline and take the first road right. A .45 mile pedal on hard-packed dirt brings you to the dam. Here the waters from First and Second lakes flood the lowland, creating habitat for waterfowl. If you are a bird watcher as well as a biker you may decide to take this route in the early morning or evening when your chances for seeing birds are greatest.

A gradual uphill pedal along the same road returns you to the Circle Route. This is a short trip - seven miles in all - and a good tour to take before you start traveling or after a day of driving in the car.

A view from the Waterfowl Nesting Site on Drummond.

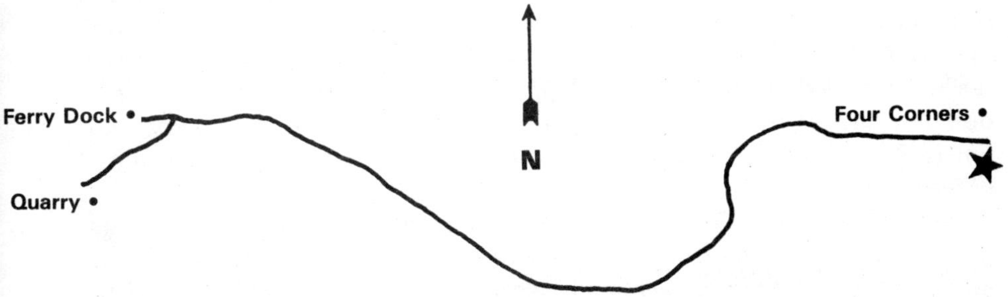

Route 4 - Quarry Route

- •Excellent
- •One-Way
- •7 Miles
- •Even Grade
- •Paved

The Quarry Route begins at Four Corners and stretches for seven miles along the island's main road to the Ferry Dock and dolomite quarry. The paved road is predominantly gentle slopes with a few moderately steep grades. You will find more car traffic here than on the other routes because the road is especially busy when the ferry docks. This is a one-way route. You must return to Four Corners on this road.

Leaving Four Corners bike west out of the village. You'll pass a few houses and businesses but you'll soon leave the town's activity behind as you bike along the wooded roadside. This route is a blend of the scenic aspects of Drummond Island attractive to tourists and the everyday work life of the island necessary to the islanders. About four miles from the village you bike along Pigeon Cove, another secluded area good for fishing. It is also very scenic so you might want to stop your bike for a minute and look out across the cove to Sturgeon Bay.

Soon after leaving Pigeon Cove, you glimpse a long straight road on your left. The road is paved with crushed white rock and bordered by large white boulders. It looks like a railroad track without the rails. This is the service road to the dolomite quarry and you will keep it in sight as you bike the rest of this route.

Just past the ferry dock is the entrance to the quarry. Because it's secluded from the rest of the island, you may be surprised by the extensiveness of the operation. This quarry, established in 1942, is one of the largest industries in the eastern section of Michigan's Upper Penninsula. Three million tons of dolomite are shipped from here each year. The dolomite, a very hard limestone rock taken from this quarry, is used for making steel, cement and other products.

Throughout history other limestone has also been quarried on the island. Rock from Drummond Island was used to build the locks at Sault Ste. Marie and for fireplaces in homes and cottages throughout the area. Tours of the quarry are arranged by request, so if you want to see the quarrying in progress, stop at the office and ask to be shown around.

The quarry is located on the site of Fort Drummond, the last British stronghold in this area. The British abandoned the fort in 1828 and today only one smokestack remains to remind us of the past. This only visible ruin is on private land, however, and not accessible to the public. The quarry has taken over the rest of the fort site and the grinding of drills and truck gears has replaced the clicking of swords and tapping of feet as the British paraded on these limestone cliffs. We can only imagine what it must have been like for them as they guarded the channel from these sun-washed rocks before abandoning the site to the modern age. You may want to linger here awhile, observing the quarrying or watching the ferry load and unload, before you return along this route to Four Corners.

The quarry road, bordered by large white boulders, runs along the main highway on Drummond.

Big Shoal Bay Beach encircles a beautiful secluded cove. In this quiet spot, Kathy takes a rest from biking.

ST. JOSEPH ISLAND

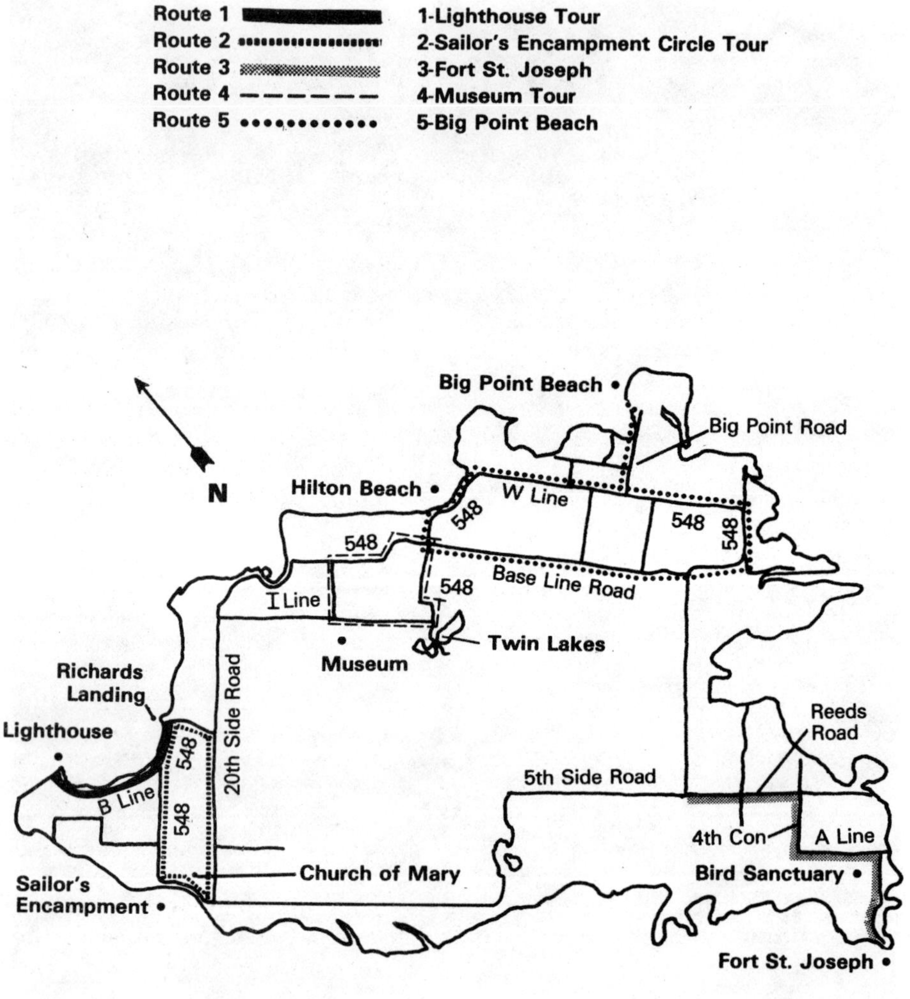

St. Joseph Island

Located in the North Channel connecting Lake Superior with Lake Huron, St. Joseph Island is an unspoiled wilderness retreat. Miles of country roads cut through dense maple forests, making the island especially popular with vacationers who want to "get away from it all."

To reach St. Joseph Island take Trans-Canada Highway 17 east from Sault Ste. Marie on the Ontario side. Twenty-eight miles from Sault Ste. Marie turn right onto the free bridge leading to the island. The bridge makes the island easily accessible from the Canadian mainland and you can come and go here according to your own schedule.

St. Joseph Island was first settled by the British in 1796. When Jays Treaty of 1794 required the British to evacuate Fort Michilimackinac, they chose St. Joseph Island for their new location. Fort St. Joseph was built in 1796 and occupied until the War of 1812, when the British recaptured Fort Michilimackinac.

Today the fort remains a major center of interest, but St. Joseph Island has other attractions as well. One of these is its extensive maple forests. In autumn the brilliant oranges and reds of frosted leaves are a feast for the eyes; in spring the maple sap, cooked to a clear amber, provides a feast for the stomach. In both seasons St. Joseph's "sugar bushes" attract visitors.

The island's maple syrup industry dates to the early days of island settlement. In fact, in 1834 one million pounds of maple syrup was shipped from St. Joseph Island. Worth $75,000, this syrup rivaled the waning fur trade as a major force in the island's economy. Today St. Joseph maple syrup attracts tourists for a festival in the spring and continues to bring travelers throughout the summer as the syrup remains on sale in the island's shops and private homes.

Although not as profitable as maple syrup, the Pudding Stone is another natural attraction of St. Joseph Island. These round, speckled stones can be found on beaches and in fields throughout the island. A mixture of red and brown colors, the stones reminded the early English settlers of pudding cooked with currants and cherries, so they nicknamed this rock Pudding Stone. You may want to watch for these unusual stones as you bike the routes on this island.

St. Joseph Island provides an adventure in wilderness biking. The island is sparsely settled and most of the roads are gravel. In some cases just a mile or two of pedaling from a village takes you to remote wilderness roads. Although the scenery is beautiful, especially when you bike through the maple woods, the roads often make biking difficult. Loose gravel on the hills may hinder your control of the bike and sharp stones on the level grades may

A good map of St. Joseph pointed our way to the lighthouse near Richards Landing.

put extra wear on your tires. Before biking the island, you will probably want to read our descriptions and ratings of the routes carefully and select those routes - or parts of routes - that match your biking skill and interest. We have planned five routes on St. Joseph Island for a total of about forty-eight miles of biking.

Route 1 takes you from Richards Landing to the lighthouse 3.9 miles away. This one-way route can be combined with Route 2 which is a circle tour of the southwestern end of the island. Route 3 takes you 7.7 miles through wilderness to Fort St. Joseph. You must either drive to the starting point at the eastern end of the island or connect Route 3 with a route of your own planning. Routes 4 and 5 begin at Hilton Beach. Route 4 is a circle route through peaceful countryside to the island museum. Route 5 is also a circle route. It takes you on excellent paved roads to Big Point Beach, then circles through remote wilderness on the return to Hilton Beach. Depending upon your interest and experience, you may want to bike this as a one-way route. Follow the paved road to the beach; then when you are ready to enjoy the beach, return to the village the way you came.

St. Joseph Island is one of the most underdeveloped islands we biked. Like Beaver Island, it has many unimproved roads through remote wilderness areas. We thoroughly enjoyed biking on St. Joseph Island, but we took precautions to insure safe trips. We always carried food and water. We biked during the cool time of day. We carried maintenance kits for bike repairs. We also knew our biking limitations. Some of these roads, especially those described in the circle tour of Route 5 are better suited to off-road bikes and wilderness biking enthusiasts.

Plan carefully for these trips and match the route to your individual biking style. Then relax and enjoy biking this charming wilderness island.

Kathy records the beauty of a picturesque lighthouse on St. Joseph.

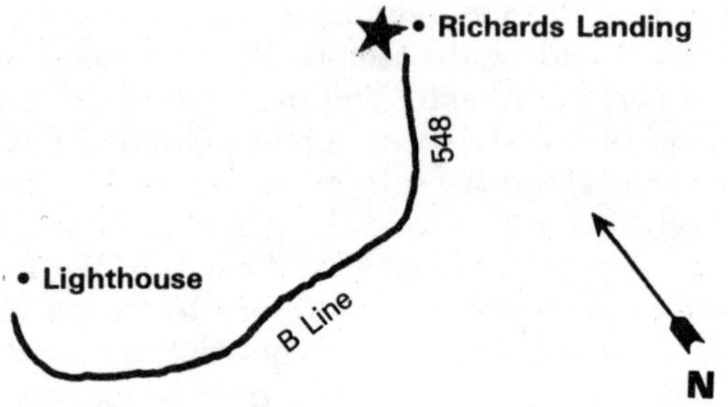

Route 1 - Lighthouse Tour

- •Very Good
- •One-Way
- •3.9 Miles
- •Even Grade
- •Paved/Dirt

This 3.9 mile route begins at Richards Landing, one of the island's two villages and takes you around St. Joseph Channel to a picturesque lighthouse. The road is an even grade, about one-half paved and one-half dirt. Although the dirt is soft in places, overall the route is very good biking. We biked this one-way route in early evening after a long day's car ride. The eight mile round trip along this peaceful island road was a soothing end to our day.

Richards Landing is a pleasant village with a library, a grocery, motels, and restaurants. A store featuring an excellent collection of Canadian Indian art is located along your way out of town. Richards Landing also has a marina and a pleasant park near the waterfront where you can rest or enjoy a snack before starting this route. From Richards Landing bike south out of town on Highway 548 for 1.2 miles. This paved road is moderately uphill at first, but soon levels off for a fast ride through beautiful countryside. Pleasant woodlots and wide meadows line both sides of the road.

Bikers enjoy some solitary evening biking on St. Joseph's 548.

Turn right on B Line and bike 2.7 miles to the lighthouse. At first, you'll pass small farms, but as you near the lighthouse the farms give way to cottages and lake-front homes. The road follows the shore closely here so you have a good view of the channel.

The narrow dirt road ends at the edge of the water and we enjoyed the feeling of biking to the farthest point of land. In the middle of the channel at the tip of a long rocky finger of land perched a squat, white lighthouse. Accessible only by boat the light guarded the channel and warned boats away from the rocky shoreline.

The stillness of this picturesque setting inspired us and we lingered here as the setting sun cast a rosy glow against the wooden walls of the lighthouse. Finally, we turned our backs reluctantly on this narrow finger of land and returned the way we had come to Richards Landing.

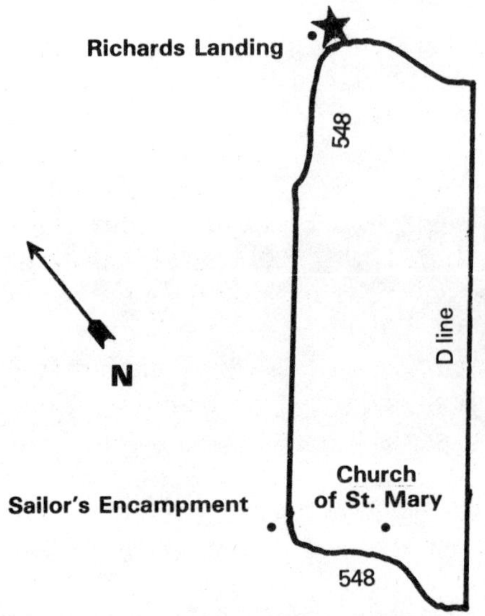

Route 2 - Sailor's Encampment Circle Tour

- Excellent/Good
- Round-Trip
- 8.7 Miles
- Hilly
- Paved/Gravel

This 8.7 mile circle tour takes you along one of the island's most beautiful country roads to Sailor's Encampment, a narrow channel where freighters pass on their way from the St. Lawrence River to Lake Superior. Highway 548 to Sailor's Encampment is paved and excellent biking. You may decide to make this a one-way route and return to Richards Landing on the same road. If you want to bike the circle route, you will return to the village on D Line. Loose gravel combined with hilly terrain makes biking somewhat difficult on this road. If you bike the entire route, use caution on D Line. You may also decide to combine Route 1 to the lighthouse with this tour. Bike south from Richards Landing to B Line. Turn right on B Line for a side trip to the lighthouse; then return to the main road to complete the tour.

Start this tour at Richards Landing and bike south 1.2 miles to B Line. Here you can turn right for a side trip to the lighthouse (see Route 1) or continue about 2.5 miles to Sailor's Encampment. The paved road to Sailor's Encampment is excellent biking. Moderate inclines lend some challenge to the otherwise effortless pedaling. We biked this route during a long summer evening. The late evening sun warmed the old log structures and cast a golden glow across the overgrown fields along this route. Cattle grazed on the hillsides and our bikes seemed to be the only mechanical invention in the quiet countryside. Caught up in the beauty of the evening, we sat high in our seats and let the warm breeze rush past our faces. Riding a bike on rural roads during a late summer evening is a special pleasure.

We coasted down a gradual incline and followed the road around the coast. A low rock fence bordered the field on our left and the river channel curved gracefully on our right. We didn't see any freighters in the channel, but boats moored along the shore added charm to this already picturesque scene. We biked slowly along the shore savoring the quiet appeal of Sailor's Encampment.

Just ahead on your left you will see a small white church perched on a high hill overlooking the channel. Built in 1876, Church of Mary is the first church on the island. We parked our bikes at the base of the hill and climbed the steep hill to the church. Delicate blue forget-me-nots spread across the lawn and mingled with the cemetery markers behind the church. We sat on the wide, green lawn and looked out across the water. From our vantage point, we could see far across the open water. From the hilltop the church seemed to guard Sailor's Encampment, helping to provide safe passage for the ships traveling here. Their location seemed especially appropriate for the simple, white church

A low rock fence bordered a field along Sailor's Encampment on St. Joseph.

When you are ready to leave this scenic spot, you can either return to Richards Landing from here the way you came or continue on to D Line. If you decide to complete the circle tour, bike east on 548 until your reach D Line. You'll bike up a steep hill bordered by evergreens, then soon you'll see D Line on your left. Turn onto the gravel road and bike 3.8 miles on a straight stretch of country road. Modern farms mingle with toppling log structures and split rail fences for an especially scenic route. The road is quite hilly, however, and loose gravel complicates biking here. Use caution on the short steep hills. Loose gravel can make coasting quickly a precarious venture here. You may also find biking up these hills taxing because of the loose gravel. Take your time and concentrate on your biking while you enjoy the special beauty of this rural setting. We found ourselves stopping at the top of some of the hills to enjoy the panoramic view. Meadows bordered by woodlots stretched in all directions and we savored the stillness of this pastoral setting.

All too soon it seemed, we reached the end of this quiet backroad. Although we were somewhat relieved to pedal on blacktop again, we were reluctant to give up our country biking.

When you reach Highway 548, turn right and bike 1.3 miles on excellent paved road back to Richards Landing. Large maples along this route remind you that St. Joseph Island is a maple syrup center. "Maple Syrup for Sale" signs along the road also indicate a bountiful spring harvest. Tempted by the thought of fluffy pancakes smothered in maple syrup we stopped for a jug of the amber liquid. Then we biked quickly toward our cottage with our treasure safely stowed in a bike pack. As the sun settled in the west, we enjoyed a late night feast, confident in the feeling that our country bike ride had earned us this special treat.

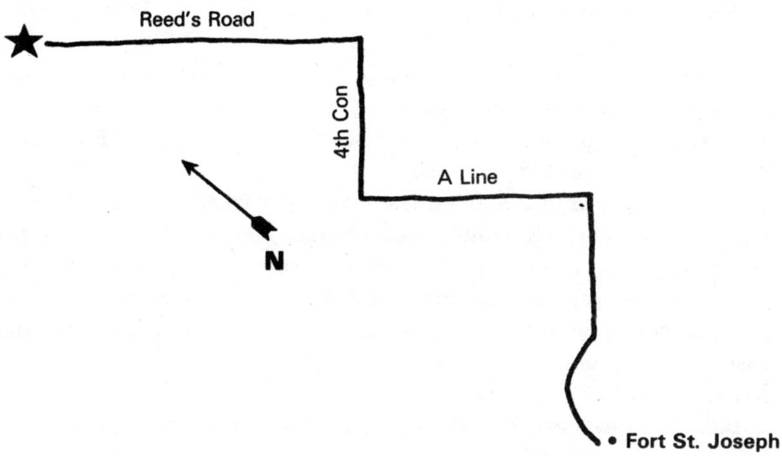

Route 3 - Fort St. Joseph

- Very Good
- One-Way
- 7.7 Miles
- Even Grade
- Paved/Dirt

This route begins at Reeds Road and winds 7.7 miles through wilderness to Fort St. Joseph. You'll bike on good roads through a bird sanctuary to the farthest southeastern tip of the island where the fort is located. This one-way route is predominantly level grade and very good biking.

We began this route where Reeds Road branches off from the main highway. We had been driving the perameters of the island and decided to get away from our car and do some biking. Reeds Road seemed like an attractive backroad and a good place to start. You may also decide to drive to Reeds Road and park your car along the shoulder of this country road; or you may include this route as part of other bike trips of your own planning. Whichever way you decide to take this route, we think you'll appreciate the solitude of biking in this remote area.

Starting at Reeds Road bike east 2.6 miles to 4th Con. You'll see a few houses and one country church on this route, but you will bike mostly through a wilderness setting. A sign in front of one driveway especially impressed us with the remoteness of the area. It said: "No admittance except for water." We felt like pioneers exploring primitive territory. Automatically we checked our water supply. Reassured by a full water bottle, we biked on more confidently.

Turn right on 4th Con and bike 5.1 miles to the fort. Here you'll pedal through dense wilderness, the last two miles of which are bird sanctuary. The birds were relatively silent the day we biked this, but we did see a furtive mink-like animal hurrying across the road in front of us. If you are bird-watching enthusiasts, you may also glimpse a rare bird to make this trip especially memorable for you.

About thirty minutes from the time we parked our car at the junction of Reeds Road and Highway 548 we arrived at the fort. After immersing ourselves in wilderness biking, the modern headquarters for the National Park Service was a bit of a surprise. Probably the original fort was also an isolated center of activity in the remote wilderness setting. But according to historical accounts, one soldier called the location "the military Siberia of Upper Canada."

Built in 1796, Fort St. Joseph was a British outpost. When according to the treaty of 1894 the British were forced to give up their fort on Mackinac Island, they moved to St. Joseph Island. From here they conducted their fur trade with the Indians and protected their Canadian colonies. Although the fort was near good canoe routes from the Mississippi and the lower Great Lakes region, the British continued to prefer Fort Michilimackinac and during the War of 1812, they reclaimed their fort on Mackinac Island. Again, however, a treaty caused the British to abandon stragetic location for a fort. They passed up St. Joseph Island this time and built their fort on Drummond Island. When you bike Mackinac, Drummond and St. Joseph Islands, you can follow the adventures of the British military during the height of the fur trading days.

Built in 1796, Fort St. Joseph is now the site of a national park. Travelers can walk around the restored ruins of the fort.

Today you can sit in a comfortable theatre at the National Park Headquarters on the site of Fort St. Joseph and watch films of the voyageurs and early fort life. A small, but excellent museum also helps you understand what life was like here in the early 1800s.

After touring the headquarters, walk the short distance to the fort site. Although only foundations of the original buildings remain, a tour booklet helps you picture the original fort. You can stand on this beautiful point and look across the lake in three directions. It's easy to imagine the merry bustle of voyageurs and the precision of British military personnel at the height of the fur trading days. After touring Mackinac, Drummond and St. Joseph, we decided the British had a special talent for selecting the most beautiful locations for their forts.

When you are ready to leave the fort site, you must return to Highway 548 the way you came.

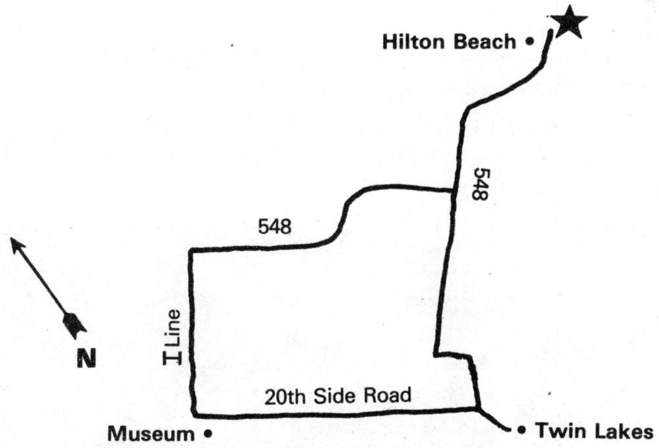

Route 4 - Museum Tour

- Good
- Round-Trip
- 8.7 Miles
- Moderate to Hilly Grade
- Dirt

Beginning at Hilton Beach, one of the island's two settlements, this circle route takes you through 8.7 miles of quiet countryside to the island's museum. A short side-trip to Twin Lakes gives you a great excuse for a picnic before returning to Hilton Beach. Although most of the roads on this route are dirt, they are good for biking and the beautiful backroads scenery more than makes up for any inconvenience you may find when biking dirt roads.

Begin this tour at Hilton Beach and bike .6 mile south away from the village. You may think the steady uphill climb is a brisk way to begin a tour, but keep pedaling - you will soon be on level ground. At the top of the hill, Highway 548 turns right. Follow this road and bike east 2.2 miles. This is the island's main highway and a direct route from the bridge to Hilton Beach, so you might meet some traffic here. It is a good paved road, however, so both bikers and drivers can use the route together. You'll bike past some houses here. They are spaced far between and surrounded by woods. Even though you are on the island's main thoroughfare, you'll bike mainly through rural settings.

2.2 miles on this road brings you to I Line. Turn left here and bike south to the museum. This level dirt road cuts through lowland. Some fields and houses mix with the evergreens to make a varied terrain. We saw a young mother pushing a baby carriage here, so we didn't complain about the road's surface for biking. Although there are some loose patches of dirt, I Line is good biking.

1.3 miles on I Line brings you to a four corners where 20th Side Road crosses I Line. Here the museum is located on two sides of the road. You'll see a church on your left and a school, barn and house on your right. The buildings are authentically restored and depict island life from the 1700-1800s.

St. Joseph Island Museum features authentically restored buildings from the 1700-1800s.

The museum is surrounded by wilderness and the buildings must look much the same as they did two hundred years ago. We lingered here, sitting on the church steps and imagining ourselves back in time. There must have been many high points to life in the 1800s, but we were glad to be part of the present. Without regret, we mounted our modern bicycles and continued our tour through the backroads of St. Joseph Island.

From the museum, bike 2.1 miles east on 20th Side Road. This is a beautiful backroad. Impressive hardwoods border the road on either side; in places they spread their branches toward each other to form a leafy canopy over the road. We didn't see any houses on this road, so we were able to immerse ourselves in wilderness biking.

When you are ready to leave Twin Lakes, bike back the way you came on Hilton Road, but this time when you reach the intersection with 20th Side Road, bike past it and continue north on Hilton Road. This is a narrow tree-lined road with some steep hills and loose gravel. But you can again bike under leafy canopies through unbroken wilderness, so if you like rural roads, you should enjoy biking here. Two miles from the intersection you will meet Highway 548 at the top of a hill. This is the same incline you biked up when you started this route. Now you have earned the rapid downhill coast into town. Have fun!

A short side trip to Twin Lakes adds another dimension to the Museum Route.

This is the end of Route 4. But if you are ready for more biking you can pick up Route 5 here for pedaling to Big Point Beach.

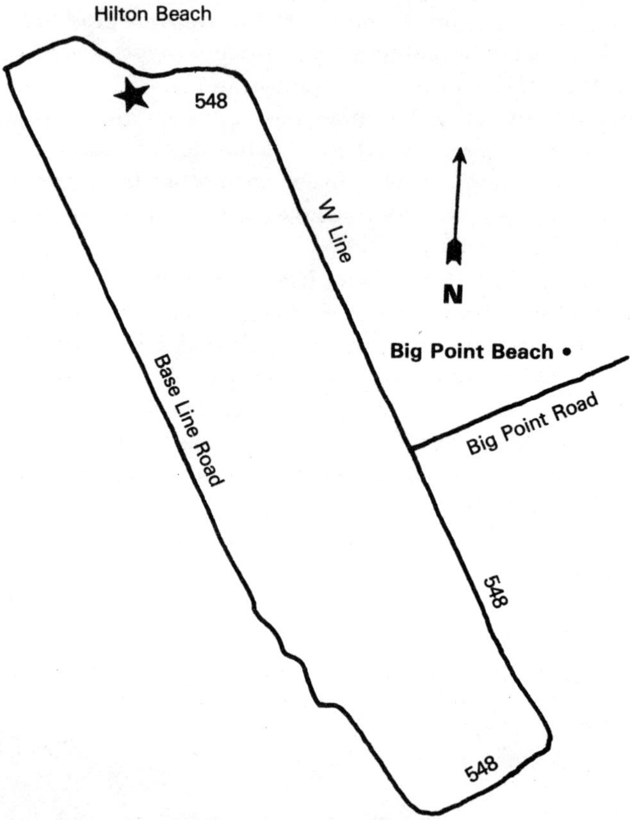

Route 5 - Big Point Beach

- Excellent/Poor
- One-Way/Round-Trip
- 6.2/19.4 Miles
- Even Grade
- Paved/Gravel

This one-way route takes you from Hilton Beach to Big Point Beach, a public beach with picnic tables and children's play area. Most of the 6.2 mile route is excellent biking on paved roads, but the last 1.4 miles on Big Point Road is very difficult biking because of the loose gravel.

If you are a skilled and energetic biker, you may also decide to make this a 19.4 mile circle tour; start at Hilton Beach, bike to Big Point Beach, then return on unimproved Base Line Road to the village. Although the scenery is beautiful along this route, loose gravel on the roads makes biking slow and difficult here. We biked the circle route, but we recommend the entire tour only to experienced, hearty bikers. Take plenty of food and water with you because you will be biking through some of the island's most primitive wilderness. If you have an off-road bike or are especially attracted to wilderness biking, we think you'll enjoy the circle route. If you are using a touring bike and want a pleasant half-day jaunt to the beach, we recommend the one-way route on W Line.

Starting at Hilton Beach, bike northeast out of town. A long uphill pedal takes you past a few houses and summer cottages, but you will soon leave these signs of civilization behind. The paved road winds through dense wilderness, broken occasionally by collapsing log buildings from another time.

4.8 miles from town turn left on Big Point Road. This dirt road has some steep hills just as you turn onto it, but it soon levels off. The loose gravel and holes make this road difficult biking, however, and we found ourselves walking our bikes through some of the more difficult terrain. A 1.4 mile pedal brings you to Big Point Beach.

Big Point Beach is actually a sand spit extending into Lake Huron. Water reeds grow along the beach, occasionally trespassing on the sandy shore. A few picnic tables on the beach itself indicate that people probably spend more time picnicking than sunbathing or swimming here.

Big Point Beach is a sand spit extending into Lake Huron.

When we visited this beach in early June, carp were spawning in the shallow water just offshore. The huge fish splashed and frolicked among the reeds and we enjoyed watching them while we ate lunch. We were the only people in the area and we were easily caught up in the wild beauty of this Canadian wilderness.

When you are ready to leave the beach, you may decide to return to Hilton Beach the same way you came, for a total round trip of 12.4 miles. Or you may also decide, as we did, to continue east on W Line for a circle tour through some of the island's unspoiled wilderness.

If you choose the circle tour, turn left where Big Point Road meets W Line and bike east. This paved road soon becomes dirt. When we biked here, some road construction was evident, and we speculated that this stretch might soon be paved. At the time, however, the loose dirt made biking difficult here. W Line becomes 548 and curves around Mosquito Bay. You'll bike through some bottom land here with cedar and hemlock providing a pleasant change of scenery. 5.4 miles from where you left Big Point Road you'll see the sign to Base Line Road. Turn right and bike west for 5.8 miles. This is one of the most beautiful wilderness roads we biked, but the loose gravel makes "slow-going" here. Maybe that's an advantage; you can take time to enjoy the sights of mature hardwood forests on both sides of the road.

The silence of this wilderness area settled around us and soon we were conscious only of the crunching of our tires on the gravel as we spun slowly along. We don't remember seeing a house on this road, but we do remember feeling some reluctance to return to paved roads and the civilization at Hilton Beach.

Base Line Road is a level grade, shaded from the sun by impressive hardwoods, so if you are an experienced biker who enjoys wilderness biking you should find this route a good addition to your tour of the island.

When Base Line Road meets Hilton Road, turn right and bike .6 mile north to Hilton Beach and the end of your tour.

In early June you might see Carp spawning off Big Point Beach.

Loose gravel on St. Joseph causes biker to ride with care here.

MANITOULIN ISLAND

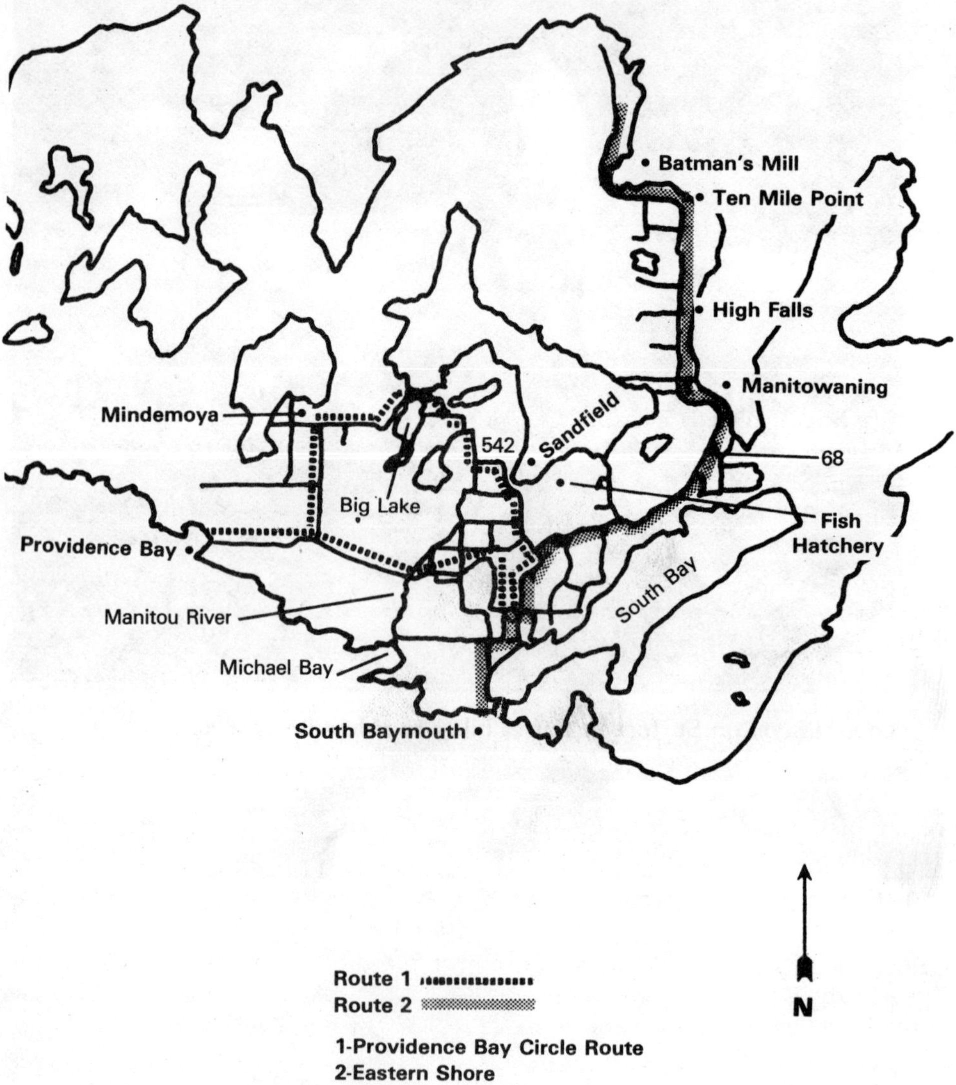

Manitoulin Island

Located in Lake Huron, Manitoulin Island stretches for almost one hundred miles along the top of Georgian Bay. As the largest fresh water island in the world, Manitoulin is an appropriate home for the Indian's Great Spirit, Manitou, who according to Indian legend, makes his home on the island. Although Manitoulin is large, you are never very far from water when you travel here. The island has more than eighty miles of shoreline and one hundred inland lakes. The width of the island varies from two miles to forty miles and on a map it looks like many tiny islands clinging together.

To reach Manitoulin, travel east from Sault Ste. Marie on Trans-Canada Highway 17 for two hundred thirty miles. Turn right on Highway 68 and follow this road about fifty miles to Little Current, one of Manitoulin's largest settlements. Highway 68 runs along a short peninsula and across a small island before reaching Manitoulin, so you will probably feel like you are hopping from island to island. With water on both sides of you, you'll drive through rocky bluffs outlining dense forests. This very scenic highway is a good introduction to the beauty of Manitoulin Island.

Although the scenery on Manitoulin is beautiful, bikers will probably be most impressed by the roads. Manitoulin's roads are excellent for biking. The routes we have planned for you combine wilderness settings with paved roads of even grade. On Manitoulin we biked on excellent roads through quiet countryside, the perfect combination for biking.

We have planned two routes on Manitoulin, totaling eighty-nine miles. Route 1 is a circle tour beginning at South Baymouth. On this route you'll bike through peaceful, rural countryside to Providence Bay, Manitoulin's longest sand beach. Route 2 is a one-way route along the island's eastern shore. Although this route is along the island's main highway, the traffic flow is light and the landscape is beautiful. You can stop at High Falls and Ten Mile Point for scenic views and visit Batman's Grist Mill for a glimpse of the island's past. Both routes offer a variety of interesting stops and appealing scenery.

The only disadvantage casual bikers may find on their routes is the long distances from place to place here. Because the island is larger than the other islands we biked, the routes are also longer. The circle route from South Baymouth to Providence Bay is fifty-five miles and the one-way route along the eastern shore is thirty-four miles. Even hearty bikers will need a full day if they plan to bike the entire route.

Split rail fences add to the scenic beauty of Manitoulin Island.

You may decide to bike these routes in stages. You can start anywhere you want on the route and bike as far as you want in one day. Another alternative is to stay overnight along the way. You can bike to Manitowaning or Providence Bay, for example, stay overnight and complete the route the following day. Adapt these routes to your biking preferences and we're sure you will enjoy biking Manitoulin Island.

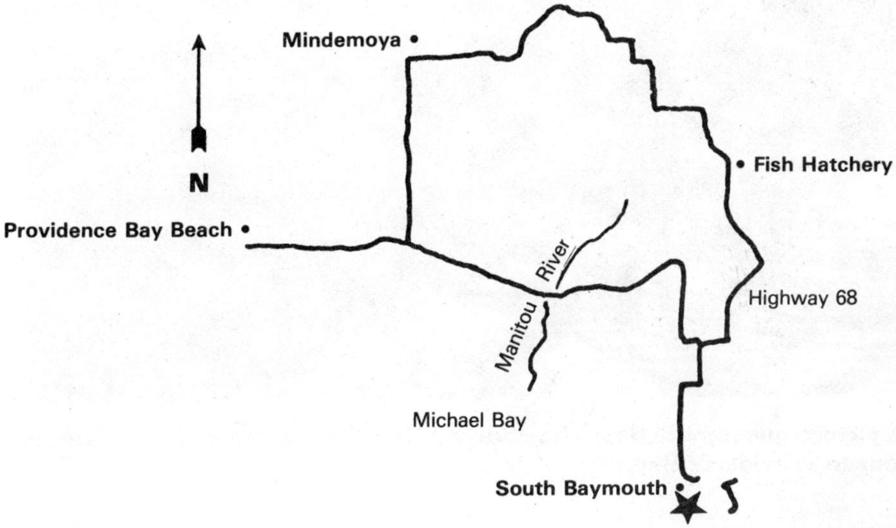

Route 1 - Providence Bay Circle Route

- Excellent
- Round-Trip
- 55 Miles
- Moderate Grade
- Paved

This fifty-five mile circle route takes you through some of Manitoulin's most scenic countryside. Split rail fences outline fields of white daisies and log buildings blend with woodlots and pasturelands. Every bend in the road seems to offer a new picture, but the scenery is only one of the exceptional attractions on this route. The roads are also excellent for biking. Paved, even grades combined with light traffic let you immerse yourself in the pleasures of biking. Good paved roads and remote countryside are difficult to find together, but when they occur, as along this route, they provide exceptional biking.

A picturesque scene in South Baymouth marks the beginning of this beautiful tour to Providence Bay.

Although you can bike this entire route in one long day, you may choose to take this tour a variety of ways. Even on excellent roads, fifty-five miles is a long pedal, and we recommend it only to experienced bikers in excellent physical condition.

If you would rather bike a shorter distance, you can plan to stay overnight somewhere along the route. There's a motel at Providence Bay and at Mindemoya as well as campgrounds and cottages along the way. Pack extra clothes and a picnic lunch and plan two days for biking this route. You can also choose to bike only sections of this tour. Take your car to some location on the route and set out from there; then return to your car when you have biked your fill. Whether you bike the entire route or just a part of it, we know you'll enjoy the experience.

As we biked here, the sun warmed our backs, a breeze cooled our faces and everything came together to make this an exceptional biking adventure. We wish you a similar experience as you bike the Providence Bay Circle Route.

This route begins at South Baymouth, a cluster of stores, restaurants and motels catering to tourists who use the ferry service from here to Tobermory on the mainland. From South Baymouth bike northeast on Highway 8. This is a wide, paved road with some moderate uphill grades cutting through rocky outcroppings. You may also meet some traffic here, especially if you bike this near the time the ferry docks.

Three miles from South Baymouth turn left at the sign "Providence Bay Park." You will not see a road sign from this direction, so your only landmarks are the sign to the park and the distance from the village. You'll have to watch closely so you don't miss the turn.

Now you'll leave the traffic behind and bike through the kind of quiet countryside that has made Manitoulin such a popular island for biking. Soon after we left the main highway, we coasted down a hill and biked through a river valley. Willow and alder shrubs bordered the stream, sheltering it from casual view. But someone obviously knew the stream well because as we biked past it we spied a row boat hidden in the reeds near the shore. The bow of the boat jutted into the water as though waiting for someone to push it into the main current and head toward the bay for another kind of island adventure.

After you cross the stream, the terrain gradually changes from dense wilderness to open meadows and cultivated farmland. Split rail fences border the road here, enclosing fields of white daisies and outlining farmyards. A few gradual hills will keep your mind on biking, but for the most part you can speed along on this paved even grade and let your thoughts drift.

Rugged beauty is typical of the landscape along the road to Providence Bay.

Pedal 3.9 miles on this road, then turn left to Providence Bay. A green arrow points the way, but it is almost hidden by trees, so watch closely for it. Now you are on a straight stretch to the bay. Although the pastures are a bit more rocky here, the exceptional scenery continues. Sun-warmed logs stretch in zig-zag borders along the road and rise in sturdy structures across the landscape. Woodlots and fields mingle to provide varied scenery along this fourteen mile route. We stopped where the Manitou River crossed the road and scanned the distance to where the river emptied into Michaels Bay and Lake Huron beyond. This is one of the few places you can see Lake Huron while you bike this route.

The entire distance from South Baymouth to Providence Bay is 20.9 miles. The last couple of miles as Kathy pedaled slower and slower, Larry called encouragement. "It's all downhill from here," he said optimistically. In reality, it was not "all downhill" but the thought made the last two miles go more quickly and eventually we pedaled smoothly into town on roads of even grade.

Providence Bay has the longest sand beach on the island. Curving white dunes billow and mount near the road, hiding the beach from view. But a short climb to the top of the dunes brings you to a panoramic view of the beach. White sand, stretching for as far as you can see on either side, gives plenty of space for beachcombers and sunbathers to enjoy this peaceful place.

At first we biked past the dunes and into town to stock up on picnic supplies at the country grocery. But, eager to enjoy this long stretch of sandy shore we returned quickly to the beach. We parked our bikes at the base of the dunes and hiked over the soft mounds toward the water. A brisk breeze blew off the lake, so we settled against one of the dunes to eat our lunch. Sheltered from the wind, we grew warm and drowsy in the sun. After the long pedal we had earned our rest. But eventually we pulled ourselves from the sandy cushions and let the brisk lake breezes tease us fully awake before returning to the road to see more of the island.

You may decide to linger in Providence Bay. If you are beach wanderers as well as bikers, you can spend hours here. There's a campground across from the beach and a motel in town, if you want to spend the night here. When you do decide to continue this tour retrace the route 5.8 miles to the road to Mindemoya. Turn left and bike 5.2 miles through island wilderness to Mindemoya, one of the island's largest towns.

When we biked here, the first mile was in very poor condition because of a washout, but that area was under construction so hopefully the road will be in better condition when you bike it. The rest of the route was good dirt road of even grade. Lowland woods and marshes mingled here, and Larry kept looking for a moose in the long stretches of swamp land. But if there were moose in this area they didn't show their heads. Only the bullfrogs boomed greetings to us as we biked along. Although we didn't see the bullfrogs either, we did see a lot of wild irises blooming in the ditches. The bright blue flowers stood out vividly against the greens and browns of the marsh, and although Larry may have been disappointed in the lack of wildlife, Kathy was perfectly

Larry kept hoping to see a moose along this wilderness route.

happy to "settle" for a glimpse of the flowers.

Just beyond the long marsh you'll see the settlement of Mindemoya. A large town, by the island's standards, Mindemoya has good shopping and complete medical services. There are stores, restaurants and service stations here. This is another place where you can rest along this lengthy route.

When you are ready to leave Mindemoya, bike east on the road to Sandfield. This 12.4 mile route takes you through peaceful countryside to the island's fish hatchery. Along this paved route the farms are larger and more modern than they were along the road to Providence Bay, but split rail fences still border the fields and wild irises grow in the ditches. We took our time here, enjoying the bright green fields outlined against a cloudless blue sky. Both the weather and the scenery combined to make this route exceptional biking.

Streams and lakes were common sights along this route. They seemed to be preparing us for a visit to the fish hatchery. The road curved around Big Lake, lying like a piece of glass in a field, and dipped toward Long Lake before twisting through the countryside to Sandfield. We struggled up a steep hill, then coasted past Manitou Lake, the largest lake on the island, to the fish hatchery.

Here a pleasant picnic area tempted us to stop for another lunch before we toured the hatchery. Two men wound a large fishing net on a storage frame as we walked along the river bank. Large trees shaded the bank while delicate blue forget-me-nots clustered along the shore and flourished in the river sloughs and shallow places. Near the river, lake trout, bass and brook trout swim in ponds until they are large enough to be released in the island rivers and lakes. A tour of the fish hatchery is an interesting side trip to this bike route.

When you leave the fish hatchery you are 11.6 miles from the completion of this circle route. Continue through Sandfield and up the hill out of town. You'll bike 3.6 miles on excellent paved roads to the main highway. Prosperous looking farms line both sides of the road here and you may meet some traffic along this road as you near the highway.

Knowing we were nearing the end of our route, we picked up speed and enjoyed the sheer pleasure of the aerobic exercise. Pedaling fast, we soon reached the main highway. Here we turned south and pedaled eight miles back to South Baymouth. Quiet cabins nestled in the evening shadows and stillness settled around us as we biked through dense forests and beneath rocky ledges. Finally, tired but relaxed by the intense exercise we completed the circle route. We had covered fifty-five miles and we could say with certainty that Manitoulin Island offers some of the best biking on the Great Lakes.

Manitoulin's main highway is excellent for biking.

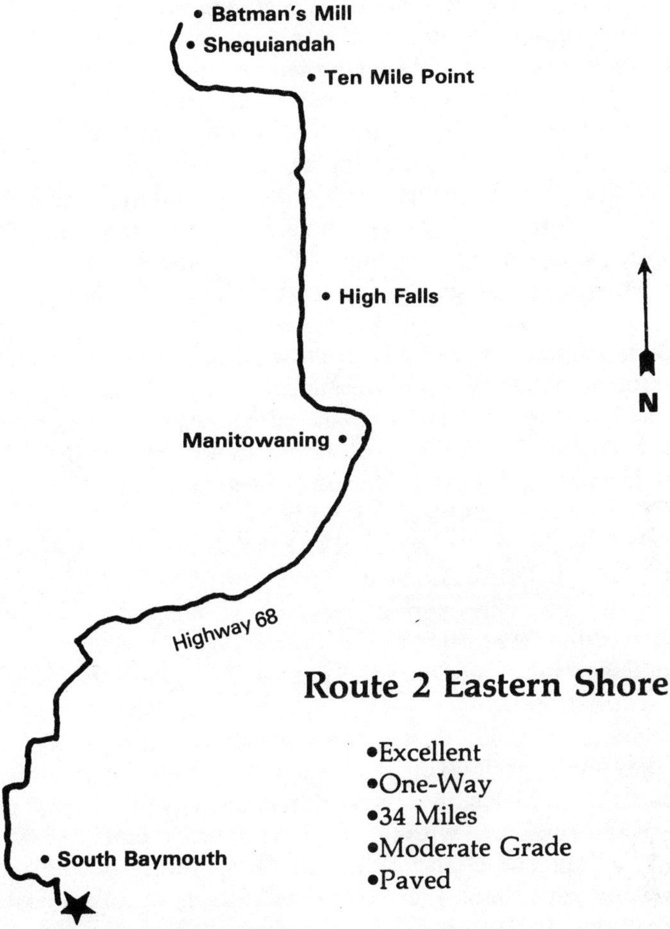

Route 2 Eastern Shore

- •Excellent
- •One-Way
- •34 Miles
- •Moderate Grade
- •Paved

This thirty-four mile route from South Baymouth to Sheguiandah takes you along the eastern shore of the island. You'll bike through quiet countryside from the busy ferry dock at South Baymouth past an impressive waterfall to a restored grist mill at Sheguiandah. You can bike this one-way route all in one day if you have transportation waiting for you in Sheguiandah, or you can divide the route in half and bike from South Baymouth to Manitowaning the first day and continue on to Sheguiandah the second day. There are resorts and motels in Manitowaning if you decide to stay overnight.

This route also connects with Route 1 eight miles from South Baymouth so you may want to join them to make a more lengthy bike trip of the island. The paved road is predominantly even grade and excellent biking. You can go all out for the exercise here or bike slowly and enjoy the scenery. Either way, we think you'll enjoy this tour.

This tour begins in South Baymouth and covers the first eight miles of Route 1; from there you continue on to Manitowaning, another 9.9 miles of biking. Although this is the island's main highway, we met very little traffic when we biked here. The paved, level road is excellent for biking.

We biked this route in early evening. The setting sun sent our shadows stretching toward the split rail fences bordering the road. As we watched ourselves spin silently along the highway, we understood the intense satisfaction of long distance touring. "I could bike forever," Larry said. Modern farms lent a special beauty to this route. The evening sun slanted off the green-roofed barns, and sea gulls covered the tilled fields like late spring snow.

All too soon it seemed, we reached Manitowaning where we stayed for the night. A quiet town on the bay, Manitowaning is - according to Indian legend - the home of the Great Spirit, Manitou. The name means "Den of the Spirit" and Manitou is said to live in the area. As we looked out across the clear, blue waters of Manitowaning Bay, we found it easy to believe that the Great Spirit would have chosen this place for his home.

Perhaps appropriately, the oldest church of the Manitoulins is also located here. Built in 1945, St. Paul's Anglican Church of Canada is located across from the lighthouse on a cliff overlooking the bay. We parked our bikes on the lawn and tried the front door to the church. To our surprise, it swung open slowly and we walked into the small chapel. This place, too, seemed appropriate for a Great Spirit.

You may decide - as we did - to stay overnight in Manitowaning or, after a look around the town, continue on to Sheguiandah. When you are ready to leave Manitowaning, take Highway 8 north from town and bike 5.8 miles to High Falls. This is a rural area with farms lining the road on either side. Beef cattle roamed behind stone and split rail fences and sea gulls circled overhead. Two donkeys shook their long ears at us as we biked past.

About a half hour pedal from Manitowaning you'll see the sign to High Falls. Turn right and park your bike near the picnic grounds; then you can follow the fenced path to the falls. Feeling a bit weak-kneed we peered over the cliff to watch the water cascading into the stream below. With relief, we returned to our narrow-wheeled touring bikes, and the more "solid" experience of biking on firm ground.

When you leave High Falls continue for 5.6 miles to Ten Mile Point. Stop here and take some time to enjoy the scenery. From the lookout, you can see across the sheltered bay. We met a biker from Germany here. On his way to Little Current to spend the night, he planned to tour more of Canada before returning home. He was only one of several long distance tourers we met in Manitoulin.

High Falls is one of the scenic stops on this eastern shore.

The view from Ten Mile Point is spectacular.

If you are growing weary of pedaling, you will enjoy the next section of this tour. Almost immediately after leaving Ten Mile Point you will start down hill. This is the longest slope either of us has ever biked. We just coasted and coasted practically into the Indian village of Sheguiandah. If you plan to return the way you have come on this one-way route, you may worry about getting back up the hill. But when we returned, we were surprised to find how easily we could pedal up it. This is such a gradual slope that it is as much fun biking up as it is coasting down. So sit back and enjoy your long coast down this gradual grade.

4.2 miles from Ten Mile Point we biked through Sheguiandah on the Indian Reserve. Just past the village at the base of the hill, we turned right and biked .7 miles to an old grist mill near Bass Lake. As soon as we turned off the main road, we could hear rushing water and we knew the mill had to be just ahead. Following split rail fences, we biked up a short hill and crossed a small bridge to the mill.

Built in the 1800's Batman's Mill has been recently restored. Although the wheel is still silent, you can picture the water rushing from the sluiceway and the great wheel turning to grind the island's grain. The brown wooden mill blends into the backdrop of hills and trees. Standing on a flat rock that spread across the churning water, we marveled that industry could have once taken place in such a scenic spot.

You may want to linger here, enjoying the sounds of rushing water and resting on the sun-warmed rocks before returning to the road. From here you can return the way you came to Manitowaning or continue on to forge new tracks of your own.

Built in the 1800s, Batman's Sawmill has been recently restored.

Select a good bike for your island adventure.

Bikes

Although bikes have been a part of the world's transportation system since the Walk-Along was introduced in 1790, they have changed greatly over the years. Surprisingly, the addition of pedals to the Walk-Along - which was really a tall, large-wheeled scooter - took seventy years. But once pedals were added the interest in bikes prompted changes in bike design. By 1873 the first all-metal frame appeared, holding together the High Wheeler, still ridden today as a curiosity in parades.

From that development, changes became still more rapid. Only seven years later the safety bicycle appeared with wheels of the same size - the first bike in the modern sense. During the next ten years, rubber tires, tandems, ball bearings, coaster brakes, cushion saddles and adjustable handlebars were added. Four million people in the U.S. rode regularly by 1896, with factories producing a million bikes a year. So it would be easy to conclude that the bicycle must have been perfected many years ago.

The truth is that bikes continue to be improved. Many of these improvements have been inspired by racers and long distance touring enthusiasts. They have demanded faster, stronger shifting; drag-free bearings; wider gearing ranges; more comfortable clothing; stronger tires; better safety equipment; more comfortable seats and grips; and, above all, lighter and stronger frames. Industry has been responsive, offering bikes that are technological masterpieces. Will they be improved? Of course. We have scarcely seen the beginning.

In this chapter we will suggest some factors to consider as you select a new bike or adjust the bike you already have for touring the islands.

Selecting a Bike

With so many bikes to choose from, you may wonder what criteria to use when selecting a bike. To make the selection process easier, we have divided the bike into frame and component parts. In this section we will offer suggestions about what to look for in each of these areas.

Start with the frame, the basic tubular metal structure that holds everything together. You might wonder why the frame is so important when it has no moving parts. The reason is that manufacturers choose all the rest of the components - brakes, shifters, hubs and cranksets - to match the quality of the frame. Inexpensive component parts weigh more than better components. An inexpensive frame is heavy, too, so when inexpensive parts are added to an inexpensive frame, the resulting bike is too heavy for comfortable riding. If you start doing more riding and want to improve the quality of your bike, you can always add better components to a good frame. But all the best components will not improve the quality of a poor frame. You will still end up with a heavy, hard to ride bike.

So how can you spot a good frame? You should consider three points when checking the frame. First is seamless tubing built from 1018 or 1020 high carbon steel or chrome-moly steel, which is stronger. Names like Reynolds, Columbus, Vitus, Ishiwata are standards of excellence in tubing. The lightest frames are specified as built of double-butted tubing, but straight gauge tubing is adequately light for all but top level racing at a much lower cost. You might also select an aluminum frame at a higher price still, with a resulting lower weight.

The second point to look for is the construction at the frame joints. Lugs are like sockets that fit around the tubing sections where the vertical and horizontal pieces meet. While there are some excellent bikes built without lugs, the majority are lower in quality, and you will improve your odds for a good frame by selecting one built with lugs (they are not found on aluminum frames). If you find a frame built of chrome-moly tubing lacking lugs but specified as Tig welded, it will be at least as strong and light as a lugged frame.

The last point to look for is the smoothness of the brazing or soldering around the lugs or joints. Good workmanship will be shown by smooth, even brazing. If you look for quality steel or aluminum tubing and a smoothly built lugged or Tig welded frame, you will have a base that will carry all the best components any time you choose to add them. A good frame will give you years of biking pleasure.

A triangle is stronger than a U-shaped piece of metal. For that reason, the strongest bikes are always men's models or diamond frames, as they are properly called. Women seldom bike in dresses these days, so they can also feel comfortable riding the stronger diamond frame. Most women today either buy a diamond frame style or a myxte, which is a compromise between the diamond and the women's. The myxte can be recognized by its twin drop bars that slant downward to the rear axle. It gives a slight cut-out on top, but much greater strength than the true women's bike, with its characteristic curved frame. The myxte style will prevent the problem of bar height, so select the same size that fits you in the diamond frame.

One last thought on bike construction is to consider one of the new folding models. Folding bikes have been around for many years, but only recently have they become more than curiosities. Several are now so well designed that they do offer riding ease and comfort along with fast takedown and portability.

Most manufacturers match the component parts to the frame. They seldom add poor parts to a good frame because the buyer willing to pay for a good frame will not be satisfied with inferior components. So the component parts are the next point to consider. There are many manufacturers of excellent component parts. Some names to look for are Campagnolo, Sun Tour, Shimano, Huret or Dia-Compe. Avoid any components with obvious plastic parts to break or wear out sooner than metal.

Gears: One of the most important component parts is the gearing mechanism. Here are some things to consider when selecting the number of gears and type of gear shift for your bike.

You can choose from one speed, three speeds, five speeds, ten speeds and more. Avoid the one speed bikes as these normally have heavy frames and one gear is not enough to adjust to different kinds of terrain. Unless you are a real athlete, avoid racing bikes with their higher gearing and skinny tires. You will want to carry some equipment with you and the gearing on racing bikes is not suitable for carrying a load. Touring bikes have gearing specially adapted to carrying loads, so they are the most comfortable to ride with extra weight.

If your budget is limited, you might be better off with a three speed hub-shift model. Three speed models usually have lugged frames of medium quality and handle a variety of cycling conditions. They are by far the most popular bikes in Europe, where people bike as regular transportation. The three speed hub shifter is enclosed so it cannot collect dirt to wear out the parts. Even more important, the shift mechanism is less likely to be harmed if the bike falls over or is bumped. Shift mechanisms on ten speed bikes are more vulnerable to abuse, so for younger riders and anyone who likes to keep things simple, the three speed would be a good choice. For most riders, though, the ten speed touring bike is the best choice. These are available in either loaded touring or sport touring models to match your needs. The derailleur mechanisms shift easily and positively, providing a wider range of gearing than a three-speed can offer. Even the inexpensive models now feature quality tubing and alloy rims that were found only on high priced bikes a few years ago. The weight and cost have both dropped, resulting in a comfortable ride at an appealing price.

Bikes with more than ten speeds are becoming popular for heavily loaded long distance touring. They do require more adjustment during the shifting process because the sideways distance between the multiple gears is so great. With more than ten speeds to choose from, you may benefit from some lower gears than a ten speed offers.

Ten speeds are enough to handle any roads except mountain grades in the United States and three speeds will allow you to pedal most of the routes in this book, so don't assume that a bike with the greatest number of speeds will be the best choice. Instead, ask the dealer what the gear range is. Rather than ratios like 3:1 or 5:1, bike gears are usually stated in gear values, either in inches or in centimeters. A typical range is 39 to 104 inches. That is too high for comfortable touring. Try to find a bottom number of 32 or less if you plan to enjoy biking all kinds of terrain. If you find a bike that suits you in all other ways, ask the dealer to change the gear cluster to give you lower gear values.

Brakes: Gears are great for moving, but sooner or later you will have to stop. Every bike will have brakes, but some brakes perform better than others. As soon as shift mechanisms are added to a bike, the coaster brake, where the bike is slowed by pressing backward on one of the pedals, will vanish, being replaced by caliper brakes. Pressing against the wheels, caliper brakes can be used together to stop both wheels instead of just the rear one as coaster brakes do. Hand operated, they can be applied instantly with the pedals in any position, making them far safer than coaster brakes.

Caliper brakes are available as center-pull or side-pull styles. Center-pulls are recognizable by the triangle formed by the brake cables just above the calipers on each wheel. Side-pulls have, instead, only a single brake cable runnning to one side of each pair of calipers.

Not surprisingly, many experienced cyclists are convinced that center pull brakes are the best. They operate easily, resulting in smooth stops. But side-pulls give about equal stopping power. Some of the best bikes have side-pull brakes. Inexpensive bikes also have side-pull brakes. The problem is that it is expensive to build side-pull brakes that work the way they should. As a result, the less costly side-pulls have given side-pull brakes a black eye. If you are selecting one of the better bikes, you may find either side-pull or center-pull brakes.

Try to test ride the bike and see that the brakes grab smoothly when you pull the brake levers. If the pads strike evenly on both sides of the wheel and instantly return to the fully open position when you release the brake levers, either style of brake should serve you well. The ease with which the brake pads snap open when the brakes are released is the best guide to their quality. Often, inexpensive side-pulls will stop the bike well, but one of the brake pads will continue to rub against the wheel after the brakes have been released. The rubbing is often hard to hear, but extra friction will tire you more quickly. So check the brakes to be sure they release completely. A few touring bikes are now starting to appear with a third braking arrangement called cantilever brakes that give even greater stopping power. Only a few of the better touring bikes and the new all-terrain bikes now come equipped with cantilever brakes, but they may become a catchy selling point, ending as standard equipment even on inexpensive bikes. The style of brakes, then, may be no clue to the quality of the brakes on the bike itself. Only by testing the brakes can you be sure that they will work reliably.

Brakes on ten speed models are available with one set of brake levers or with two sets, the second set being below and parallel with the center part of the handlebars. Called safety levers, these allow you to apply the brakes easily when your hands are resting - thumbs toward you - on the top bar. Riders will adopt their own favorite riding position, but nearly everyone will ride at least part of the time with hands resting on the top bar. Without safety levers, it may take too long to hit the brake levers from that position to stop in an emergency. Although there is some controversy about the braking power of safety levers, we have found ours adequate, and you may want to look for a bike with safety levers.

Touring bikes have gears adapted for carrying loads. Here our bikes - ready for a day of biking - wait out the ferry ride to Mackinac.

Adjusting Your Bike

Although discount houses may offer lower prices, often their bikes come ready for assembly. You have to be a better-than-average mechanic to assemble a bike so every part fits and functions properly. Regular bike shops have the added advantage of expert assembly. For that reason you may prefer to buy from a bike shop.

For the person who is not an expert at adjusting, a properly set up and adjusted bike from a reliable bike shop could mean the difference between riding in comfort and pure misery. For example, ten years ago we bought a pair of Motobecane touring bikes from a dealer who set up, adjusted and tested our bikes. Both bikes have been ridden thousands of miles since then, but the brakes and shift mechanisms have been given only about two minor adjustments in all that time. Few things in life are as trouble-free as that. The point is that a properly adjusted bike tends to stay that way, while a badly adjusted bike will get worse in a hurry. A bike specialist with skilled mechanics is your best bet for happy cycling.

Even an expertly assembled bike will need minor adjustments. Here are some suggestions for fitting a bike to your build and riding style.

Start with the saddle height. Be sure to adjust the saddle because incorrect height can turn any ride into a torture test. To make the necessary adjustments, you will need a wrench to fit the clamp nut that locks the seat post in the seat tube. A small crescent wrench is the most convenient tool. Mathematical formulas have been worked out for this, but trial-and-error is still the best technique. Ideally, the saddle should be raised enough to allow a very slight bend in your knee when you are sitting in the saddle with the pedal down and the ball of your foot resting on the pedal. Be sure to wear the shoes you will be riding in for all adjustments. It is helpful, too, to ask someone to hold the bike vertically for you so you can test for the slight knee bend with both legs. When the height seems correct, tighten the clamp nut securely. Caution: Be sure at least two inches of the post remains inside the tube for safety.

The angle of the saddle can also be adjusted. Keep the angle close to horizontal but experiment with the angle a little above and then a little below. For some reason, a small difference in the seat angle can mean the difference between all day comfort and misery within a couple of miles. We prefer our saddles slightly below horizontal, but many people prefer them above. The adjustment is easily made by loosening the nuts on both sides under the seat, so customize your angle by trial-and-error. When you are satisfied, tighten the nuts securely.

You will notice that the tube holding the stem of the handlebars slants toward the saddle. If the handlebars are raised, they also move to the rear. Likewise, the saddle is usually built on a pair of bars that allow it to move to the front and back several inches. The reason for these two motions in handlebars and saddle is to place them the correct distance apart. With your elbow touching the front of the saddle, your outstretched fingertips should be no more than an inch from the center of the handlebar. If the distance is greater, loosen the seat nuts and push the seat forward. Raise the handlebars slightly if the length is still too great. In all handlebar adjustments, keep at least two inches of the stem inside the tube for safety. All new bikes are inscribed with a mark on the stem to tell you how far the handlebars can be safely raised. Follow the mark for an upward limit. When the length is right between the seat and bars, tighten the seat and bars securely. The bike should now be adjusted for comfortable and efficient riding. You may want to experiment with changes, because the same formula may not fit everyone's riding style. The famed cyclist Eddie Merckx reportedly often made saddle adjustments while riding in major races, so experimentation should be the rule.

A properly adjusted bike will give you many miles of biking pleasure.

Bikes can be easily loaded and unloaded from a rear carrier.

Outfitting and Transporting Your Bike

At one time or another, most of us have felt the frustration of lacking some needed item on a trip with no way to replace it. The article might have been left behind either by accident or because a shortage of packing room dictated that it be left behind. The shortage of storage space confronts bikers even more than those who travel by car or plane. The basic bike frame often seems to offer no place to tie anything. Limiting, too, is the fixed power source of one pair of legs. Motorized vehicles can be provided with extra horsepower to anticipate heavy loads, but bikers can only lower their gear ratios slightly to cope with heavy loads.

The result of this limitation is that bikers must select packing space that will distribute the weight both low and evenly. We have often passed bikers burdened by large packs on their backs, carrying gear just as they would while backpacking. The high center of gravity created by a backpack is hazardous for the biker, inviting an accident through loss of balance or control.

Equipment manufacturers have answered the demands of bikers, designing special packs to give useful carrying space where none seems to exist. Many of these are inexpensive but amazingly convenient. With a combination of small packs you will be able to carry everything you need for the trips in this book, as well as on longer tours. This section will help you decide what packs you should have, along with some ideas for the biggest carrier of all - the one that transports your bike by car.

Selecting Bike Equipment

Even on short tours you will want to carry some items, such as food, water, clothing and a few tools. With your bike properly outfitted the process is simple. When selecting equipment, buy the best that you can afford. Good equipment lasts longer and performs better. In this section we will discuss bike packs, tire pumps and other bike accessories.

Bike packs: Bike packs can be attached to just about any part of your bike. They swing from the handlebars, ride on top of the back tire or are fastened to the frame tubes on a diamond frame bike. Here are some hints for selecting the best pack for your bike and style of touring.

Handlebar bags and frame packs carry everything you need for a day of touring.

Handlebar bags attach to the bike handlebars. When selecting a handlebar bag, look for one that can be mounted without interfering with the brakes and that has downstraps that attach to the wheel hubs. A bag that ties only to the handlebars is likely to collapse when any weight is added, causing the bottom to rub on the tire. It may even flop back and forth as you ride, shifting the balance of your bike. So look for a good quality bag that can be locked down and is waterproof just in case you are caught in the rain.

If you are riding a diamond frame bike, you might choose one of the new **frame packs** designed to fit in the frame triangle. These are inexpensive, fit snugly with no sway and essentially no forward wind resistance, and hold tools, food and spare clothing without interfering with your leg action. Best of all, they are easily accessible while you ride, so you can cure a sudden attack of the munchies, deposit litter or put away extra clothes without stopping.

Probably the most useful carrier is a **rear rack** for the back. Inexpensive and lightweight aluminum racks are now available to carry any gear you are likely to need. Racks absorb objects of any shape, lashed on top with bungee cords. For example, our trips have been even more enjoyable since we found that the insulated coolers designed for the space between car seats would fit perfectly on a bike rack. The low area with indentations for beverage cans fits neatly under a bike seat of average height and the flat bottom allows the cooler to be lashed securely to the rack. It is indeed a pleasure to pull out a cold can of fruit juice, cool cheese, or fruit after a long, hot ride. These coolers are even more useful since they can be used in cars or for other picnics as well as bike trips.

With a frame pack, a handlebar bag and a rear rack, all the gear for two or three people can be carried on day trips. For one person, either a handlebar bag or frame pack will provide enough carrying capacity except for odd-sized items, where a rear rack will come in handy.

A rear rack is handy for tying on extra gear. We found a small cooler fit perfectly on the back of Kathy's bike.

Another kind of bike pack used to tote water is a **water bottle.** You will be pedaling almost constantly, burning off calories but also losing water from sweat and evaporation. A water bottle attached to the lower frame will provide you with a drink to prevent dehydration. Some bikes are factory equipped with braze-ons on the frame to help attach water bottle holders, or "cages" to the frame. Cages can also be bolted on with mounting clips that are provided for bikes without braze-ons. One water bottle is enough for day trips for most people but if you are a "heavy drinker" you can always add a second bottle. Be sure to carry at least one, though, because some of the island routes will take you through wild country with no drinking water available.

Always carry water when touring these islands. Here Larry stops for a drink on Beaver.

Tire pumps: While bikers run on food and water, bikes run on air. If you don't believe that, just try riding a bike with a flat tire and you will find out. To prevent finding out the hard way, you should plan on a method for maintaining proper pressure in your tires. There are several options.

The first is to buy a good quality **hand pump,** attach it to the frame and add air whenever your tires drop below the suggested pressure marked on the side of the tire. If you choose this option, try to avoid the inexpensive plastic pumps. The pump itself may work fairly well, but the end attachments may blow apart at about forty pounds of pressure, which is not enough for most bike tires. Plan to spend at least ten dollars for a pump that will work. You will also need a tire gauge to check the pressure you have pumped.

Larry uses a hand pump to put air in a tire.

Another approach is to buy a **foot pump** that has a built-in gauge. These cost about ten dollars and will pump ninety pounds of pressure in a few strokes. But they are too large and heavy to carry on a bike, so you will have to inflate your tires before each ride and hope you don't need air before you return. Actually, if your tires are in good condition the chances that you will need air due to a leak, puncture or blowout are very small on day trips.

The only tire problem we encountered while riding all the routes in this book was a blowout, resulting from an old, worn tire. But the bike coasted safely to a stop, so no one was hurt. By inspecting your tires for worn spots and large cracks, you should be able to prevent blowouts. With a new tire and tube ready to put on and the tools and ability to change the tire, you should be able to cope efficiently with a blowout.

On the other hand, not everyone may want to change a high pressure bike tire. Sometimes they can be very stubborn to force on and off the rim. As an alternative to pumps, flats and blowouts, you might want to add Eliminator™ airless tubes to your tires. These hold no air at all, so they can never go flat or blow out - something to think about for guaranteed peace of mind at a slight increase in wheel weight.

Another technique that will help prevent flat tires is to add Mr. Tuffy strips inside your tires. These protect tires from punctures even when they are driven over a solid line of tacks - good insurance against flats.

Unless you use Eliminators™ though, you may need a pump, either the hand style that goes with you as you ride or a foot pump that will be used before each day's biking. The one thing to avoid is inflating your tires at service stations with air pumps designed for auto tires. It is risky to inflate bike tires accurately with power pumps without causing a blowout. If you must inflate at a service station, use very short bursts of air and check the pressure constantly with a hand gauge as you are filling each tire. Don't rely on the automatic pressure gauges built into some power pumps, as they may be inaccurate enough to cause blowouts in high pressure tires.

A foot pump is handy to use for inflating tires before you start a tour.

Bike accessories: Even though your properly inflated tires may be holding the road, your body must stay in contact with the bike at just three points: the saddle, the handlebars and the pedals. Since your body has so little contact area with the bike, you should try to get the most out of your contact. One part of the bike that will receive constant use and bodily contact is the **saddle.** Comfort on your posterior can mean the difference between an enjoyable ride and downright torture. So pay attention to the saddle. These are not terribly expensive, so if you find a bike that suits you in all other ways, you can easily have the saddle changed or change it yourself in about five minutes.

Three speed bikes and ten speeds designed for riding to the store and back or around town on short trips usually have upright handlebars. These are easily spotted by the molded handle, usually rubber or plastic, on the end of each handlebar, the rest being bare metal down to the stem where the bars attach to the frame. If your hands are held in the upright position, little of your weight will be supported by your arms or hands. With most of your weight pressing on the saddle, the posterior requires a soft, shock absorbing structure so you will find large padded saddles with mattress type springs on bikes of this style. While these are comfortable to sit on, they reduce riding efficiency by interfering with leg action and creating a bouncing sway that soaks up energy better used for turning the pedals. Still, for trips of only a few hours like most tours in this book, a mattress saddle is satisfactory.

Even with the best bike equipment, a biker gets tired. Here Kathy cools her feet in the soft sand on an isolated beach.

If you plan to link several tours together or take longer trips, however, you will find your comfort increases with a leather saddle. These are narrow and look uncomfortable, but they comform to your shape after a while and allow you to pedal more efficiently with no bounce or sway. You may see racers using nylon or plastic saddles for lightness, but these materials are uncomfortable on longer trips. Racers are concerned about winning and they can't win a race in comfort anyway. Nylon and plastic will never conform to your posterior shape; even worse, they are waterproof so any perspiration is held against your skin, causing chafing on long trips. The saddle choice, then, should be limited to mattress styles for upright handlebars and firm leather for dropped bars on ten-fifteen speed bikes. If you remain uncomfortable after several days of short test rides, add a Spenco saddle cover. They cost about twenty dollars, but measured in miles of comfort, they are practically free. Bicycling is great fun, but it is hard to smile with a sore posterior.

Probably the most important contact point is your feet, since the power to move the bike is transmitted through them. Your feet also become a crucial part of your balance, so your feet must remain firmly on the **pedals** as you ride. Three things will help you pedal efficiently. First, choose rat trap pedals with "teeth," to grip the soles of your shoes. Second, wear appropriate biking shoes and third consider adding toe clips to your pedals.

Toe clips hold the foot securely on the pedal.

Toe clips consist of a metal toe support to prevent your foot from sliding forward and a leather strap around your foot to prevent it from sliding to either side. Toe clips are often used by bike racers and long distance touring cyclists because they allow the biker to pedal more efficiently. On the other hand, toe clips require a bit of agility and practice to slide your feet into and they can be a nuisance if you are stopping constantly to admire the scenery, rest or take photos. You might reach your conclusion about toe clips from this: If you are reasonably athletic and comfortable on a bike, give the toe clips a try. But if you seldom bike, and feel a bit shaky on a bike, avoid toe clips until you are more experienced. They are easily bolted or unbolted in a minute or so on rat trap pedals, so you can try them, then change your mind at any time.

The last contact point with the bike is through your hands. Where they touch the **handlebars**, you must have a firm, dependable gripping surface. The handlebars are built from metal tubing that would be very hard on your hands. Some handlebar styles are designed for use with molded grips at the ends. If your handlebars are of this type, be sure the grips are attached tightly so they cannot twist or come off when you are climbing hills. If necessary, remove them and glue them in place with a rubber based cement like Pliobond.

Most of the handlebars on adult bikes are designed to be covered nearly all their length so you can vary your hand position anywhere on the bars. The choice of covering can make quite a difference. You can choose from soft foam, hard foam, plastic, cloth, leather, cork or combinations of these. The handlebar wrapping is easy to do and takes only a few minutes, so you are not bound by the wrapping currently on your bike. Most of these wrapping materials work well, but you might want to keep two points in mind. The soft spongy foam pieces designed to be lubricated in soapy water and slid over the handlebars may wear out quickly where your hands rest most often. Larry wore out a set in less than a month. Even worse, they soak up water in a sudden rainstorm, dissolving the soap and becoming mobile on the bars.

At the other extreme is the shiny plastic wrap. Properly applied, this will never move, regardless of the weather. It provides a rigid grip under all conditions but it, too, has a drawback. If you ride very far without the biking gloves discussed later in this book, your hands will become sore from contact with the plastic. Unless you plan to wear gloves at all times, plastic wrap is best avoided.

With two handlebar coverings eliminated, you are left with hard foam, leather, cloth and cork, all of which provide a good feel of the road, absorb enough moisture to keep your hands from becoming sore, and stay put in any weather. Many riders are bothered by sore wrists from road shock against their hands. If you want to reduce road shock with a material that will last, look for the handlebar coverings made by companies such as Spenco or Grab On Products. They are slightly more expensive than other wraps, but their flexible inner core soaks up shock. They can be slid into position by using rubbing alcohol as a lubricant. When it has evaporated, they don't move again.

If you plan to apply new wrappings, either unwind or cut off whatever is on the bars. Before you apply new wrapping, check to see that the brakes are in the best position for you. If you are planning to use foam grips, you will have to remove the brakes completely to insert the center sections anyway, so that is a good time to experiment. The screw that holds the brakes in place is usually inside the brake mechanism. It is concealed by the brake handle, but you can see it by pulling the brake handle down and peering inside. A narrow screwdriver will just fit around the brake cable to loosen the screw.

Brake location, like saddle adjustment, is another area for experimentation. Test to see where the brakes are easiest to reach from the location where you usually rest your hands. An emergency stop is no time to find that the brakes should have been somewhere else. Slide them up and down and also try tilting them slightly outward. Many riders find them faster to apply in that position. When you are satisfied, tighten the screw firmly.

If your replacement wrapping is adhesive backed, you can start winding from the bottom of each bar, wrapping with a good overlap - about one-half the width of the tape - until you either reach the center of the bar or run out of wrap. If your wrapping is not adhesive backed, you must start about two inches from the handlebar stem and wrap down to the bar ends. When you reach the bar ends, leave about two or three inches of tape and shove it inside the end of the bar. Then pound in a bar plug to hold the tape in position while it covers the ends of the bars so you don't get cut. Your new grips should then be ready for a test ride. How do they feel?

Somewhere on the handlebars you should mount two accessories that will be invaluable at times and might even save your life. These are a **light** and a **horn**. You might not need a horn on the wilder islands like St. Joseph and Beaver, but on the more populated islands a horn comes in handy. A horn calls attention to your presence and will help prevent accidents.

Light and horn combinations are available and these work acceptably. Most experienced cyclists choose battery operated models, rather than adding generators to their bikes that cause extra drag on the wheel. Any extra drag means you will be that much more tired by the end of each trip. Even worse, generators stop running when you stop at a stop sign, so any accessories operated by your generator will stop, too.

If you really want the world to take notice when you blow your horn, you can mount one of the small freon gas horns on your bar. Some cyclists prefer these, as they can be removed from the bike and carried to scare off bothersome dogs or even people. But they are too loud to give subtle hints that you are there and could panic some riders into foolish actions. For most downtown areas you are safer with a simple buzzer. Be sure it is mounted so you can locate the button in a hurry or you may as well rely on your own voice. The least expensive bar mounted lights do have a tendency to fly apart when you hit a bump. Seal the joint where the plastic faceplate joins the body of the light with strips of plastic tape to prevent a roadside battery hunt.

The light is not for riding after dark. Bike lights are not bright enough to show the road a safe distance ahead of you at night. Instead, you should turn on a light well before dusk starts to settle in because cyclists are hard for drivers to see at that time of day. You can make yourself much more visible with a light - either a handlebar mounted model or an arm or leg light that can be seen from both directions. Campers often prefer these since it can double as a camp flashlight.

If you have selected a good touring bike and equipped it properly, the last thing you want is bike theft. The islands in this book are probably as free from theft as any place you will ever find. Still, you should take all possible precautions. You will also be traveling through other parts of the country to reach the islands and may be leaving the bike on the car while you eat or shop. So a small investment in a **bike lock** may pay a high return by discouraging a would-be thief you will never meet. Undoubtedly the best locks are the u-shaped metal ones made by companies such as Citadel or Kryptonite, because these require a cutting torch to remove.

Always lock your bike up when you leave it to go sight-seeing.

The solid metal locks are expensive, so you might prefer one of the many cable or chain link locks. Although they are not as secure as the solid locks, they do require some time and effort for thieves to remove and their flexibility allows you to lock the bike to a car rack more easily.

Whichever you choose, the best locking system involves locking as much of the bike as you can. If you will be gone for a long time or are in a high-theft area, remove the front wheel and lock it with the back wheel to the frame. If there is any solid object to lock the whole bike to, be sure you do it. Parking meters, courtesy bike racks in town or the carrier and bumper on your car can all be effective. A little extra time spent locking and unlocking your bike could mean the difference between a pleasant trip and a serious loss. The more valuable your bike is, the more tempting it will be, so plan accordingly.

Transporting Your Bike

You will probably be transporting your bike to the island by car or van. Some people carry bikes inside a camper, but most bikes ride outside on some kind of carrier. Carriers are available for both front and rear bumpers, as well as the roof. Most of them work well, but before you buy a rack, you might want to consider several factors. First, do you need just a bike rack, or will you be carrying skis, surfboards or other items as well? If you plan to carry a variety of equipment at different times, you may want a roof rack that has detachable pieces to carry other kinds of equipment.

If your car has a luggage rack on the roof, you may already have an ideal bike carrier. All you have to do is adjust it so the center section of each handlebar rests on the front crossbar of your carrier when the bike is upside down with the seat centered on the rear crossbar. Use a long bungee cord to lash the ends of the center section of each handlebar down tightly on the crossbar. Use a short bungee to lock the seat down and the bike should stay there until you take it off. We have carried bikes thousands of miles that way and have never seen one move at all. A thin foam pad under the handlebars will prevent damage to the wrapping. You should also tie a short rope through each wheel and onto the forks to prevent the wheels from turning as you drive causing unnecessary wear on the bearings.

Of course, if you plan to carry a full-size clamshell luggage carrier on the roof, you will need a different kind of bike carrier. The rear mounted ones work better than front carriers, because they keep the bikes out of your line of sight and mount more solidly on the back. The only problem comes in with hatchbacks, since these require a rack that relies on two rubber feet that rest on the rear window and two larger padded feet that sit on the metal below the window. These carriers are not supposed to damage your car, but the lower feet may not be large enough. One of the feet smashed a dent in our car from the pounding on a few rough roads.

To prevent the carrier from denting our car again, we made the following adjustments. First we removed the rubber feet from the bottom brackets and bolted on a piece of 12 x 5 inch, 1/2" plywood instead. Then we covered the plywood with one inch foam rubber where it will touch the car. With the pressure area spread out over sixty square inches, your car will not be harmed by the carrier. The bike pedal on the inside bike can scratch the car's finish, though, so cover the end with a foam block available for that purpose at bike shops. If you follow these two suggestions, the rear carrier on a hatchback will work very well. It is easier to set the bike in than a roof carrier. Stretch a bungee cord around the bike and carrier bar to keep the bike from jumping off if you hit a large bump. The bike should ride smoothly in the carrier.

As you bike these islands, "May the wind always be at your back!"

Even in summer, we dressed warmly for these island tours.

Outfitting Yourself

With the bike properly outfitted, you can turn your attention to the most important part of the biking experience - yourself. In this chapter we will suggest clothing and accessories which should increase your biking enjoyment.

The photos in this book may not always show bikers wearing the clothing and accessories recommended in this section. We have tried to describe ideal conditions. Like most bikers, we sometimes neglected to wear the most appropriate clothing. After reading this section, you should weigh your alternatives and make wise choices concerning the clothing and accessories you wear.

Clothing

Clothing is an important part of your biking enjoyment. If you are too cold or too hot, you will not enjoy touring. If your clothes bind, you may suffer from chafing for days after your ride. Responding to the increased need for good biking clothes, manufacturers have developed shorts and jerseys especially for bikers. Although these clothes may be your first choice, we have found that you can bike happily in a variety of everyday clothing as long as you keep some guidelines in mind as you select your biking clothes.

First, **choose clothing appropriate for the weather.** You will probably notice that in most of the photos used to illustrate our tours, we are dressed warmly. Although summer sun shines brightly on these islands, the air temperature is usually cool and warm clothing is necessary even in midsummer. We were comfortable wearing sweatshirts for most of these tours, and we recommend that you pack long pants, warm vests and sweatshirts for touring these islands during most of the biking season.

On warm days, we still usually chose long-sleeved shirts. When biking, long sleeves are a good choice for several reasons. First, they protect you from chills. Cool winds against a perspiring body can chill you and reduce your biking enjoyment. Second, long sleeves protect you against sunburn. Because the air is so cool on these islands, you may not be aware of the strength of the sun's rays. After a day of biking bare-armed in cool temperature, you may be surprised to find that you have a painful sunburn. A long-sleeved shirt lets you enjoy the unmatched beauty of these sun-washed islands without acquiring painful sunburn. Long sleeves will also protect you from scrapes and scratches if you fall off your bike. This is another reason to wear long sleeves when biking.

Wear long sleeves to protect against sunburn.

When touring these islands, you should usually wear a warm top. We chose hooded sweatshirts for most of the tours. Hooded sweatshirts are warm and offer the added convenience of attached head cover. They are also easily stowed away in a pack or fastened to a bike or biker as the day grows warmer. Lightweight turtleneck pullovers and sleeveless vests are also appropriate. The turtlenecks keep body heat in because they fit snugly around the neck. The vests provide warmth, but allow the biker to maneuver easily.

The second guideline to consider when selecting clothing for biking is to **choose non-binding, flexible clothing.** Soft, flexible materials are more comfortable than stiff, scratchy fabrics. Your clothes should allow you to move freely. Avoid jeans that bind and cumbersome jackets that may prevent you from maneuvering quickly enough to maintain control of your bike.

Clothes designed especially for biking fit snugly. This prevents chafing caused from wrinkly or loose-fitting clothing. It also reduces wind resistance caused by baggy clothing flapping in the breeze as you ride.

Although bikers usually wear warm tops, they often choose shorts for biking. Shorts with a chamois-reinforced crotch are especially popular because they prevent saddle sores. Shorts are popular for another reason, too. They allow you to pedal freely. If you choose to pedal in long pants, make sure you secure the pants legs tightly around your ankle. This will prevent the cuffs from catching in your bike chain. When we wore long pants, we often chose jogging pants because the elasticized cuff held the pants leg securely around the ankles. Although jogging pants may give you some wind resistance, they are flexible and non-binding; therefore, you may find them an acceptable alternative to the tights designed especially for biking.

Women should select a good sport bra like those worn by female joggers. Although it may seem like your legs are doing all the work while you sit comfortably in the saddle, your arms and torso are actually receiving quite a bit of strain. Keeping your balance on winding roads and bouncing over rough roads puts stress on the upper part of the body, too. For that reason women will be more comfortable in bras designed for support during athletic activity.

The third guideline to consider when choosing biking clothes is to **wear "breathable" fabrics.** Avoid wind and water repellant fabrics that shut out all air flow. Breathable fabrics prevent air from passing inward, but allow your body vapors to pass outward. This keeps you feeling comfortable even in cold weather. Wind and water repellant fabrics, on the other hand, trap excessive body heat inside and cause perspiration to soak your clothing. That, in turn, causes chills and discomfort. If you must select non-breathable rain gear, choose a poncho style garment which will keep you dry in a rain storm, but will not trap your body's perspiration the way a non-breathable jacket would.

If you keep these three guidelines in mind, you should select comfortable and appropriate clothing within your budget.

Accessories

Accessories such as gloves and helmets are an important part of your total biking outfit. Select accessories to increase your biking safety and comfort.

The first accessory you should choose is a **helmet.** Your head is the most vulnerable part of your body and many bicycle accidents serious enough to require hospital treatment are head injuries caused by striking the head on something after falling off or being knocked off the bike. Nearly everything you can hit is harder than your head, so it makes sense to toughen up your head with a helmet. Look for a helmet that protects the whole top of your head, not just a few areas like the helmets cycle racers often wear.

A good bike shop will be happy to sell you a top name-brand helmet such as Bell, Bailen, Skid Lid, or one of the less expensive brands. How much real difference exists is hard to tell, but if it fits comfortably and keeps the sun off your head, wear the helmet and hope you never have to test it out.

Your eyes are another vulnerable area. Cycling goggles protect eyes against injury from small stones, insects or dust. Just assume you are coasting down a hill at thirty miles per hour. A bumblebee flying at fifteen miles per hour hits you in the eye with a combined speed of forty-five miles per hour. Recall what happens to insects when they hit your car windshield at 45 miles/hour; then wear eye protection.

Sunglasses protect your eyes against strain caused by riding in bright sunlight, but they may not be as sturdy as cycling goggles. They may also reduce your vision on cloudy days or when you are biking in early evening. Consider when and where you are biking and choose appropriate eye protection. Riding without eye protection is a risk you should try to avoid.

Although your hands may seem less vulnerable than your head, you should cover them with **gloves.** If you ever do take a spill, your hands may be the first part of you that touches the road. Even at a slow speed you will skid for a long distance on the palms of your hands. Bicycling gloves are designed to place leather padding between your hands and the road. They are comfortable to wear because they are fingerless, with cool mesh backs and padded leather palms. Once you are used to biking gloves and a helmet, you will feel defenseless without them, which, come to think of it, you are while biking.

Similarly, you would feel uncomfortable while driving a car without a **rear view mirror.** Yet few cyclists use rear view mirrors even though they are in more danger from the rear than motorists. It is a dangerous omission, so add a mirror. You can choose from models that clamp on eyeglasses, those that clamp on helmets or those that mount on your handlebars or brakes. Riders usually disagree on the style that is best, but we have concluded that it may depend on your eyes. Many eyeglass and helmet-mounted mirrors require close-focusing ability, but not all eyes can do that easily. We have been pleased with a model that mounts on the brake because it is a long distance from the eye and is easily seen. But a bike-mounted mirror is subject to greater shock on rough roads, resulting in an occasional blurred image from vibration. The best idea is to find a bike shop where you can try several mirror styles before you buy one.

The last accessory you should consider is **shoes.** Your feet are the primary means of transferring power to the bike, so you should wear sturdy shoes. Choose cycling shoes with fabric or leather uppers and flexible soles. Cycling shoes for the casual biker are a cross between the traditional hard-soled cycling shoe and the lightweight jogging shoe. They allow you to bike safely and walk comfortably.

If you follow the suggestions in this chapter, you should be safely and comfortably outfitted for the road.

Biking gloves have padded palms and mesh backs. They protect your hands from long hours of gripping the handlebars. But here they also prove a pretty complement to the Queen Anne's lace on Washington Island.

A well maintained bike will give you many miles of biking pleasure.

Maintaining Your Bike

In this chapter we will discuss the tools you should carry with you when you bike these routes, and we will give directions for using these tools to make minor road repairs. The tools are lightweight and inexpensive so you can take them with you easily. The directions are presented step-by-step to make them easier to follow when repairing a breakdown on the road.

From our experience, we have also identified four usual bike breakdowns: (1) flat tire, (2) broken brake cable, (3) wobbling wheel and (4) off-sprocket chain. All four of these breakdowns can be repaired by using the tools listed and following the directions given for each breakdown.

Tools

Here are the tools we suggest for your bike repair kit.

-**Crescent wrench:** buy one about six inches long. Avoid $1.90 specials and buy a good one. It will tighten or adjust most nuts and bolts on your bike. It can even adjust spokes and change a tire for you. Don't go anywhere without one.

-**Tire "irons"**: these offer the easiest way to change a tire. The best ones come as a set of three, nest in a small rectangular box and are made of - you guessed it - plastic. (You didn't guess it? Try a plastic set and you will become a believer. They don't bend or scratch rims like the aluminum ones).

-**Tube patching kit:** look for a kit with thin patches. Some patches are so thick they can hold a patched tube far enough from the tire so it blows out.

-**Spare tube:** this can be fastened under the seat with a rubber band. If a tube blows out, it may sport a two inch diameter hole - completely unpatchable. Carry a spare!

-**Spare tire:** keep one in the car just in case a tire is damaged. New tires are seldom easy to find on the islands.

-**Tire pump:** discussed earlier under basic bike equipment.

-**Small can of WD-40 or Tri-Flo:** for lubricating small parts.

-**Screwdrivers, slot head and Phillips:** to fit any screws that may need adjustment.

-**Allen wrenches:** to fit any Allen screws on your bike. These are rare, but don't overlook the large Allen screw that holds the kickstand on, if yours has an Allen screw instead of a bolt.

-**Tire pressure gauge:** needed to check the air pressure. Don't guess, as it could cause a blowout.

-**Vise Grip pliers:** often useful where a wrench doesn't work.

-**Stiff wire or a few paper clips:** because anything can break and wire is often the only means for a temporary repair.

-**Lock-It:** to keep any nuts from working loose on rough roads.

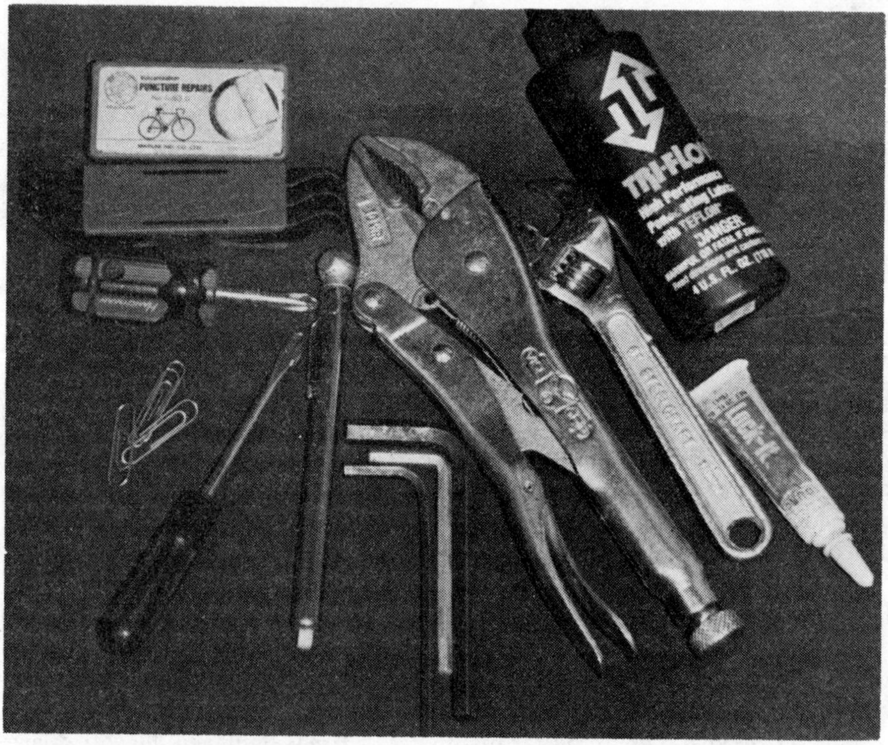

This assortment of simple tools and repair equipment will cover any of the common biking problems.

List of Tools Checklist

Do you have these tools in your bike repair kit?

- ✔ Crescent Wrench
- ✔ Tire "Irons"
- ✔ Tube Patching Kit
- ✔ Spare Tube
- ✔ Spare Tire
- ✔ Tire Pump
- ✔ WD40 or Tri-Flo
- ✔ Screwdrivers
- ✔ Allen Wrenches
- ✔ Tire Pressure Gauge
- ✔ Vise Grip Pliers
- ✔ Stiff Wire
- ✔ Lock-It

Road Repair

Now that you have assembled the basic repair tools, you can use them to fix the four most common road breakdowns. These repairs are given in step-by-step form so even an inexperienced bike mechanic should be able to complete these basic repairs.

Flat Tire

The process below covers tires for a typical ten speed bike. If you are changing a rear tire, start with step 1. For front tires, start with step 2.

1. Shift the bike into its highest gear by raising the wheel off the ground and turning the pedals while you shift up.

2. Find some means to lock the bike, right side up, to hold the wheel off the ground a few inches. You can use bungee cords to tie it to a tree, fencepost or telephone pole. If you have a friend who will hold the bike, you can try that. It is possible to tip the bike upside down but expert bikers don't do it, so use that method only if you are really stuck.

3. Loosen the nuts that hold the wheel on with your crescent wrench. If your bike has quick-release hubs, just pull the handle.

4. Work the wheel out by wiggling it sideways and slide the chain off the gear so the wheel can be removed. If the tire is too large to slide through the brake arms, either undo the quick-release lever (located under the brake arm) or loosen the adjusting nut above the brake.

5. With the wheel free, push in the valve stem of your tire to let out all remaining air. Then squeeze the tire all around where it meets the rim. Some tires fit loosely and you may be able to work the tire over the rim with your hands. More than likely the tire will be stretched drum tight so use the tire irons or the handle of your crescent wrench. Never use screwdrivers, knives or any other sharp objects.
   To use the irons, insert one end under the lip of the tire and pry downward until you can hook the lower end around one of the spokes. Then insert a second iron a couple of inches away and repeat. By the third iron the lip of the tire will be off far enough so the first iron can be removed and slid all around the rim to force the tire off. You can leave the other side of the tire on the rim while you make repairs.

Tire irons are used to pry the edge of the tire over the rim. The other end of each iron hooks over a spoke.

6. Leave the valve in place, but pull out the rest of the tube while you pump it up to find the leak. If the hole is too large to patch, insert a new tube. If the hole is too small to see, use your lips or eyes as leak sensors until you locate the hole. Be sure to mark the spot with a pen, pencil or scratch mark. Then try to find out what caused the flat. Look for a piece of glass or a tack that can be removed.
   The kind of leak in the tube will usually give you a clue about the cause. A tiny round hole was probably punched in by a small nail, where a slit was likely from glass, a chunk of metal or a stone fragment. Two tiny punctures close together that look like a snakebite were likely the result of the rim and edge of the tire pinching the tube when you hit a bump. If that has happened, keep your tires inflated to a higher pressure next time. If, on the other hand, you find a single round hole on the inside of the tube, look for a sharp spoke end that has reached the tube. Place some tape or a spare patch over the top of the spoke to prevent a reoccurrence, or sandpaper it smooth.

7. Before you patch the leak, pinch the spot with your fingers, inflate the tube again and check to be sure there are no more leaks. It is surprising how often there are two. When you are satisfied that you have found all the leaks, squeeze the air out again and rough up an area over and around the leak with sandpaper.

8. Apply a thin film of glue to the area, spreading it out quickly to cover a circle larger than the patch. Do not blow on the patch to dry it, just let it dry at its own speed. When it appears to be competely dried (about three minutes) apply a patch, being careful not to touch the back side of the patch with your fingers. Squeeze the patch with all the force your fingers can apply.

A properly patched tube is as serviceable as a new one.

9. With the tube repaired to "good-as-new" status, push it back into the tire all around and pop the tire back onto the rim with your hands as far as you can. Try to work it all the way on with your hands. If you need to, insert tire irons under the edge of the tire and pry upward, but be very careful not to damage the tube.

10. When the tire is seated all around, check the valve stem and the tube close to it to be sure the tube is not being pinched there. If you inflate the tire with a pinched tube, the tire can be forced off the rim, causing a blowout. Inflate the tire to half pressure and inspect the rim all around to be sure the tire stays seated. Then inflate to full pressure. If it holds air, give yourself a pat on the back

11. Replacing a front wheel is simple. Just push it in and tighten the nuts or push down the quick-release handle. Spin the wheel to be sure it has centered properly.

12. Replacing a rear wheel, on the other hand, takes a bit of doing. To insert the rear wheel, squat down behind the bike and slide the wheel up and forward while you pull back on the spring-loaded gear changer. Wiggle the wheel into place as you slide the chain over the smallest gear (remember, you shifted into high) and pull the whole wheel back into the slots. Something always seems to hang up, so don't be surprised if you

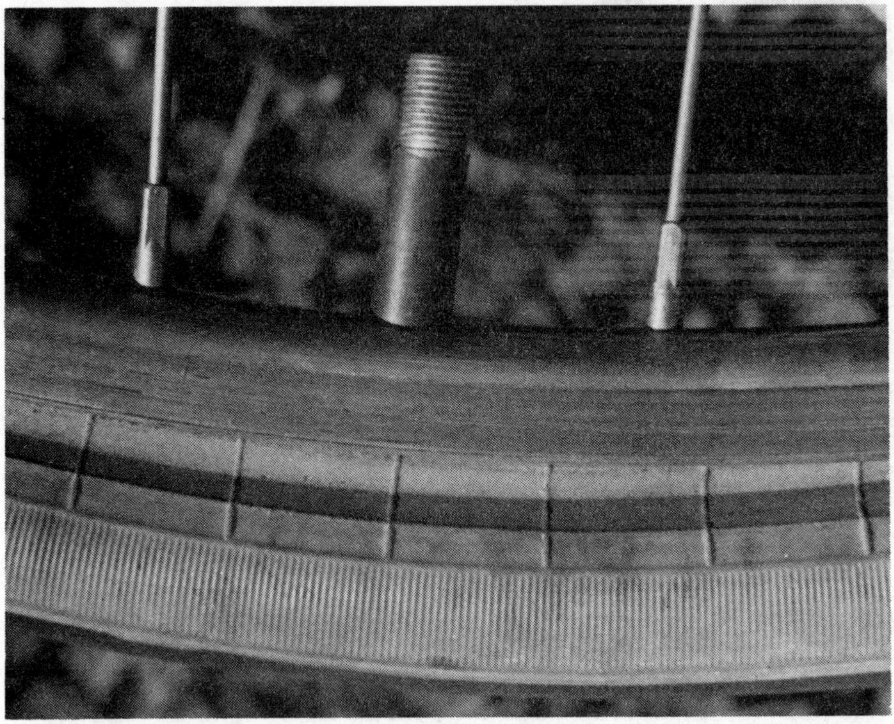

As a repaired tire is re-inflated, watch for bulges, especially at the valve stem. Follow the white area next to the rim to see the bulge under the valve stem.

have to readjust the quick-release mechanism, the brakes or something else that grabs.

A helper can be a real benefit here. When the wheel finally pops into place, tighten the nuts or quick-release handle and spin the wheel to be sure it has centered properly. If you released the quick-release lever on the brake, be sure to turn it back on or your brakes won't work right. When you are satisfied, take a short test ride, and if everything works, shifts, stops, etc., you have just joined the ranks of experienced tire changers.

Broken Brake Cable

If you have inspected the cables before the trip at the points where they rub on their housings, chances are good that any cable breaks will occur at the point where the cable fastens into the brake levers. Here, a bulb installed on the cable end fits into a socket to provide pulling power on the cable. If the bulb has been pulled off the cable, you can usually repair it with a pair of pliers.

1. Determine which brake has broken.

2. Loosen the nut that holds the end of the cable to the brake - that is, the end opposite the broken spot.

3. Pull out the slack on the broken end, and using the pliers, tie two knots in the broken cable as close to the end as you can. The knots will duplicate the missing bulb when you pull it back.

4. With the brake calipers pressed against the rim (use a helper or toe strap) lock down the other end of the cable with the nut you loosened to gain slack. Consider this a temporary repair. Replace the cable as soon as you can.

Wobbling Wheel

Leave minor wobbles until you reach a bike shop. But if the wheel has been jarred out of alignment so the bike cannot be ridden, try this:

1. Deflate the tire and remove the tire and tube. Put the bare rim back on the bike.

2. Pluck the spokes like a harp. They should all "ping" at the same pitch. Tighten any that are loose by turning the nipple counter clockwise with an adjustable wrench, or a spoke wrench.

3. Hold a pencil or a piece of chalk at the outer edge of the rim and spin the wheel to mark the high spots.

4. Tighten (one-half turn at a time) the spokes near the chalk mark and loosen the alternate spokes that fasten to the opposite side of the hub. Keep working until the wheel is round.

5. Spin the wheel with your pencil or chalk at the side of the rim to mark side-to-side wobbles. In groups of four or six, loosen the spokes next to the mark and tighten the alternate spokes that fasten to the other side of the hub. Tighten the spokes in the center of the mark more than those farther away.

6. When the wheel is true, check for protruding spoke ends that can puncture the tube. Before remounting the tire, file these off or cover them with tape or a spare patch to prevent punctures.

Off-Sprocket Chain

These directions are for the rear sprocket. For a front sprocket, the adjusting screws may be side by side, rather than over and under, and the high and low limit screws will be reversed. In front, the largest sprocket is the highest gear.

1. Pull the chain out if it has become jammed. You may have to remove the wheel to get it out.

2. Decide which adjustment screw is the one you need to turn. The rear derailleur has two screws: a low-limit screw for setting the limits of the lowest (or largest) gear and a high-limit screw for setting the limits of the highest (or smallest) gear. If the chain slipped off the largest rear sprocket, locate the low-limit screw. On most derailleurs this is the top screw. If the chain slipped off the smallest sprocket, find the high-limit screw. This is usually below the low-limit screw.

3. Adjust the proper screw until the chain stays on the sprocket. Test thoroughly by shifting several gears up and down before you ride.

The repairs described here are meant to get you back to "civilization" where you can make more thorough repairs yourself or have your bike checked by an experienced bike mechanic. Although the topic of breakdowns may seem ominous, we have experienced very few breakdowns in our thousands of miles of pedaling. If you keep your bike properly adjusted, it should run smoothly and, hopefully, you will have few opportunities to follow the guidelines for road repair mentioned in this chapter.

This is one approach to safe biking.

Bike Safety

Bikers share a common bond with all other travelers on the road: they are only as safe as the condition of their vehicles and the patterns of their driving habits allow them to be. Many highway accidents could have been avoided either by driving more carefully or by maintaining vehicles properly. To improve your chances for safe bike trips, this chapter offers some suggestions for bike safety. We begin with a safety check that you should run through before beginning each tour. We also describe an adequate first aid kit that should be part of your biking equipment, and lastly, we discuss rules of the road for safe riding.

Safety Check

Bikers should pay special attention to their safety equipment because they are often more vulnerable in accidents than drivers of motorized vehicles. Here are some things you should check before beginning to ride. Just a few minutes taken to read this list could save your life, so try to give it careful thought each time you ride.

Wheels: lift each one off the ground and spin it. Check for wobbles.

Spokes: pluck each spoke as if you were playing a harp. If any are loose, snug them up with a spoke wrench or crescent wrench. Apply the wrench to the square shank of the spoke nipple at the rim of the wheel, tightening no more than ¼ turn at a time, counterclockwise.

Spin the wheel after each adjustment to check for wobbles. Caution: with just a couple turns of a spoke nipple, you can pull the whole wheel completely out of alignment so the bike cannot be ridden.

Brakes: squeeze both brake handles and release them. The brake shoes should grab the wheels and release evenly. If either brake handle must be depressed more than half-way to stop the wheel, tighten the brake cable. Most brakes are equipped with an adjusting nut. On **side-pull brakes** you will find it just above the brake shoes; on **center pull brakes** it will be attached where the brake cable last touches the frame.

A locking ring just below the adjusting nut must be opened before any adjustments are made. To make the adjustment, depress the brake lever on one of the brakes and, while holding it, tighten the nut. You need only your fingers to turn it unless it has corroded.

After tightening the brakes, always spin the wheels to make sure the brake shoes aren't rubbing when the brake is off.

Also inspect all brake cables for wear or broken strands. Replace worn cables as soon as you can.

Tires: rotate the wheel and check all around each tire for cuts, badly worn spots, or slight bulges. Replace damaged tires to prevent a blowout.

Quick-release hubs: if your bike is equipped with these, be sure the handles are pushed down tight.

Headset: This is the joint that moves when the handlebars are turned. Test for any sign of looseness by dropping the front wheel from about 6 inches off the floor. Listen for a clanking sound. This is usually cureable by tightening the nut on top of the frame. If it still wobbles, seek help from an expert.

Light/horn: be sure these work if you plan to rely on them.

All nuts and bolts: check with a wrench to be sure each one is snug, but don't tighten so much you strip any threads.

Check the brakes to see that the calipers grab uniformly and release completely.

Lubrication: Apply WD-40 or Tri-Flow on shift mechanisms, brake levers and cables. Apply a very light coat of bike grease or 10-20 oil to the chain, then wipe off all you can remove.

After you are convinced your bike is safe, consider two final points about yourself. These may be the cause of more accidents than you might expect.

Shoelaces: especially the right one. The bow formed when you tie your shoes should be very small, tied tightly, and the lace ends should not stick out over an inch or so. If they are too long, replace the laces with shorter ones. A lace caught in the chain can turn you into a helpless falling object.

Pant cuff: especially the right one. If it is not snug against your ankle, put a band around it to lock it in place. You could use a rubber band, but this cuts off your circulation. The better way is a velcro closure pant guard from a bike shop. Regardless of what you use, be very sure the cuff can't get caught in the chain. Caught pants are extremely dangerous.

SAFETY CHECKLIST

Check these items before beginning to bike each day.

Your bike-

- ✓ Wheels
- ✓ Spokes
- ✓ Brakes
- ✓ Tires
- ✓ Quick-Release Hubs
- ✓ Headset
- ✓ Light/Horn
- ✓ All Nuts and Bolts
- ✓ Lubrication

Yourself-

- ✓ Shoe Laces
- ✓ Pants Cuffs

First Aid Kit

With your bike in safe condition you are ready to turn your attention to personal safety.

Few topics spark a discussion like the subject of first aid kits. One doctor who has biked very long distances carries no first aid material. He believes that minor problems don't need treatment and really major problems need what you won't have along. Other bikers tend to "carry it all - you never know," hoping to cover any emergency. Probably something in the middle is the best approach for most people. Here is a list of items to consider:

-4x4 gauze pads
-bandages, (assorted sizes)
-corn starch (best remedy for chafing, carried in aluminum foil)
-aspirin (if you normally use this)
-safety pins (invaluable if you split a seam on your clothing or pack or a zipper breaks)
-soap (motel-size bar useful for both normal hand/face washing and cleaning cuts or abrasions if you fall while biking on rocks or skid in loose sand while biking)
-roll of ½" adhesive tape (about 1,000 uses including repair of bodies and equipment)
-eye wash (for dust in eyes or eye strain)
-sunscreen lotion (for especially bright days)
-knife (suggested is a French country knife. They cost under $5.00 and perform any task a knife should do on a trip. They lock open and fold up for safety. Keep it sharp. A Swiss Army style knife is good, too.)
-prescription drugs you normally use
-insect repellent

Obviously, you can't expect to cope with a serious accident without all the equipment carried by an ambulance. With this list of first aid supplies, however, you will be able to handle the most common first aid situations.

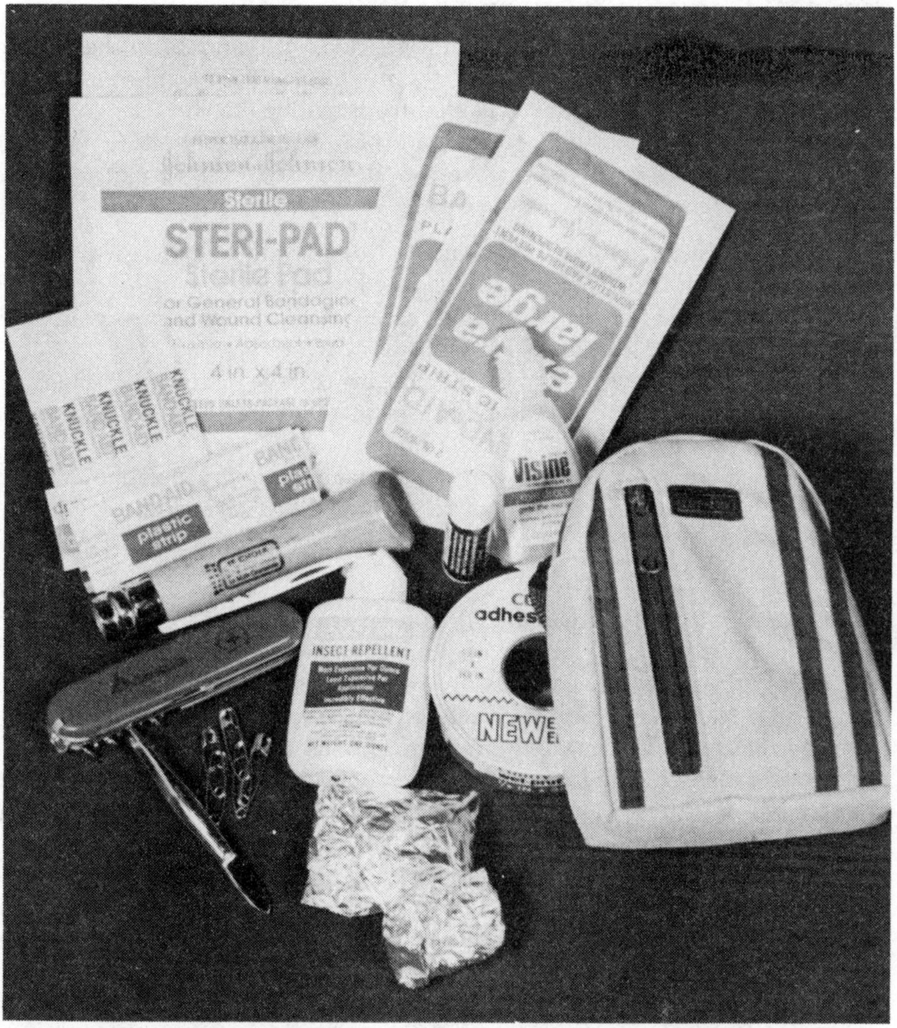

A basic first aid kit will fit into a small zippered belt bag like that on the right. Either one of the knives shown will prove useful. The Swiss Army knife may provide tweezers. The other is better for slicing fruit or cheese.

Rules of the Road

When your bike is in safe condition and you have a first aid kit for personal emergencies, you are well on the way to a safe, fun bike tour. But the way you handle yourself while you bike is also an important part of an enjoyable ride. Following are some rules of the road to consider when biking.

Ride with the flow of traffic. Bikers should ride on the right edge of the roadbed, in the same direction a car moves. Do not bike against the normal flow of traffic. Also, do not pull off the road every time a car approaches. This is dangerous because the transition from roadbed to shoulder can cause you to lose control and fall into the path of a car. The only time you may decide to pull off is when you feel "squeezed" off the road by a motorist who is unresponsive to the right of the biker.

Increase your visibility. Wear bright colors rather than earth tones, because dark colors or colors that blend with the landscape may be difficult for motorists to see. A day-glo orange safety flag on the back of your bike also increases the ease with which motorists can see you.

During early evening your visibility begins to fade. Turn a headlight on long before dark and use rear reflectors and tail lights to increase your visibility during the high risk evening hours.

Even when you have done all you can to make yourself visible, you should avoid biking in the dark. One small bike headlight or several flashing reflectors may only be confusing to the motorist. Plan to be off the road before dark.

Pay attention to the road. Daydreaming is easy on a bike. Before you know it, the rhythmic whirring of your bike has lulled you into pleasant thoughts and you are only vaguely aware of your surroundings. Try to avoid this natural reaction to biking. Watch for loose gravel, especially at intersections and corners. If you are unprepared, gravel can send you into a skid. The best advice comes from a long-time cycling friend who says, "Every time I approach an intersection or sharp curve, I think about raw meat." One careless skid and that may be what you will feel like.

Another source of danger for bikers is steep hills. Coasting down a hill at high speed is always tempting. You feel like you've earned it after the long, strenuous pedal up the hill. But biking more slowly down hills is a better idea. Stay alert and keep your hands near the brakes. Also, always keep the inside pedal up when you coast around curves to prevent it from catching as you turn. Remember, your control is limited at high speeds. If you must brake quickly, squeeze the back brake slightly ahead of the front one to prevent flipping forward.

Observe all traffic signs. Cycling accidents are often caused by careless cyclists. Don't coast through a stop sign just because you are riding a bike rather than driving a car. Use hand signals to tell other bikers and drivers where you are going, just as you would use turn signals if you were driving. Lastly, don't be lulled into complacency by the lack of traffic on many of these islands. You may have the entire road to yourself most of the time. Then, when you do meet a car, you are surprised. The car may catch you biking down the middle of the road or biking two-abreast with your touring companion. As a general rule, you should bike these island roads the same way you would bike in more heavily traveled areas.

Observe traffic signs when biking. Here Kathy stops for a stop sign.

Be prepared for bothersome dogs. Although, surprisingly, we did not meet any aggressive dogs on these island routes, you should be prepared in case you are not as lucky as we were. Some bikers carry a spray can of dog repellent made especially to use when a dog chases your bike. You can get the repellent at bike shops and carry it with you. Another way of dealing with canine harassment is to get off your bike and walk past the dog. Dogs will usually stop harassing you once your pedals have stopped moving. You can, of course, also try to outrun the dog. Often dogs will stop chasing you as soon as you are past their "territory." None of these suggestions is really foolproof in all situations. You will have to use your best judgment each time you meet an aggressive dog. Hopefully, you will meet only friendly dogs on these routes.

If you observe these safety tips you increase your chances for enjoyable, safe touring of these islands. As we said in the beginning, we hope you have as much fun biking these islands as we did, and once again we extend to you the biker's blessing: As you bike these islands, "May the wind always be at your back."

INDEX